BRAIN GAMES®

COLD CASE
PUZZLES

Publications International, Ltd.

Images from Shutterstock.com

Brain Games is a registered trademark of Publications International, Ltd.

Louis Weber, CEO
Publications International, Ltd.
8140 Lehigh Avenue
Morton Grove, IL 60053

ISBN: 978-1-64558-060-7

Manufactured in U.S.A.

8 7 6 5 4 3 2 1

Can you solve these cases?

The trail has gone cold, the criminal has gone underground, and the evidence has been packed away. But with a fresh pair of eyes and some dedication, you might just crack the case! This book provides an assortment of puzzles themed around crime and cold cases. You'll examine DNA sequences to see if they're a match, take a new look at old crime scene photos, and use logic to find long-ago witnesses. But don't stop there. Test your memory and unscramble cryptograms to reveal the details of real cold cases—some still unsolved. For variety, there are verbal puzzles where you'll unscramble quotes and solve word ladders about crimes. Some puzzles you'll solve right away. For others, you might need to set them aside for a while before returning to them. And if you get really stuck, there's always an answer key at the back. So get ready to play detective and forensic investigator, grab a pencil, and get started!

Find a Lead

Change just one letter on each line to go from the top word to the bottom word. Do not change the order of the letters. You must have a common English word at each step.

FIND

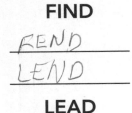

FEND

LEND

LEAD

Cold Case

Change just one letter on each line to go from the top word to the bottom word. Do not change the order of the letters. You must have a common English word at each step.

COLD

HOLD

BOLD

HOLE

CONE

CAME

CASE

Answers on page 179.

Cold Case Cryptogram

Cryptograms are messages in substitution code. Break the code to read the message. For example, THE SMART CAT might become FVO QWGDF JGF if **F** is substituted for **T,** **V** for **H,** **O** for **E,** and so on.

Fixaiir 2005 erh 2009, xli fshmiw sj imklx csyrk asqir aivi jsyrh mr sv riev Nirrmrkw, Psymwmere, wizivep mr gerepw. Figeywi xli fshmiw sj xli zmgxmqw, geppih xli Nirrmrkw 8, aivi fehpc higsqtswih, xli geywi sj hiexl gsyph rsx epaecw fi hixivqmrih. Qerc sj xli asqir oria iegl sxliv. Almpi wizivep tistpi lezi fiir evviwxih mr gsrrigxmsr amxl xli gewi, epp wywtigxw aivi izirxyeppc vipiewih jsv pego sj izmhirgi. Rs xvmep lew iziv xeoir tpegi.

The Suspect's Escape Route

You are standing at a crime scene in a building with only one exit. Elevators are local or express only; there are no stairs. What path did the suspect take to leave the building?

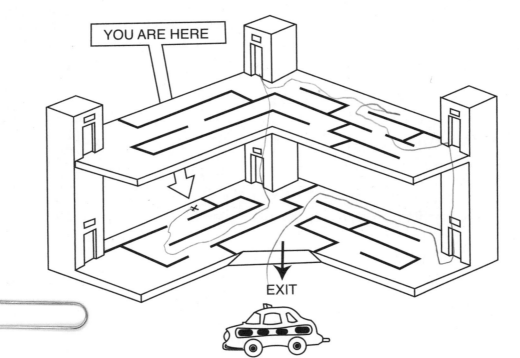

Answers on page 179.

Fingerprint Match

There are six sets of fingerprints. Find each match.

A.

B.

C.

D.

E.

F.

G.

H.

I.

J.

K.

L.

COLD CASES

Cold Case Anagrams

Unscramble each word or phrase below to reveal a word or phrase having to do with cold cases.

MERE SCENIC

LOVED SUN *UNsolved*

CUP SETS *SUSPECT*

Cold Case Anagrams

Unscramble each word or phrase below to reveal a word or phrase having to do with cold cases.

EVEN ICED

TEED CIVET

FACE STORK

Answers on page 179.

Find the Witness

On Persimmon Street, there are 5 houses. You need to find the witness on a cold case, Anjali Patel, but without any address on the doors you are not sure which house to approach. You know that Patel is a single woman who lives by herself. The staff at the coffee shop around the corner and your own observations give you some clues. From the information given, can you find the right house?

A. One member of the wait staff says Ms. Patel lives at one of the two green houses on the street.

B. Another member of the wait staff knows that a family lives in house C.

C. House D is yellow.

D. The house at one end of the street is blue; the house at the other end is white.

House A   House B   House C   House D

Answers on page 179.

DNA Sequence

Examine the two images below carefully. Are these sequences a match or not?

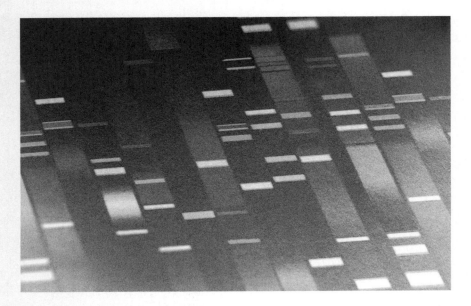

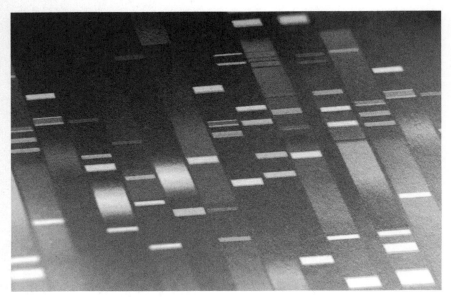

Answers on page 179.

Seen at the Scene (Part I)

Study this picture of the crime scene for 1 minute, then turn the page.

COLD CASES

Seen at the Scene (Part II)

(Do not read this until you have read the previous page!)

Which image exactly matches the picture from the previous page?

1

2

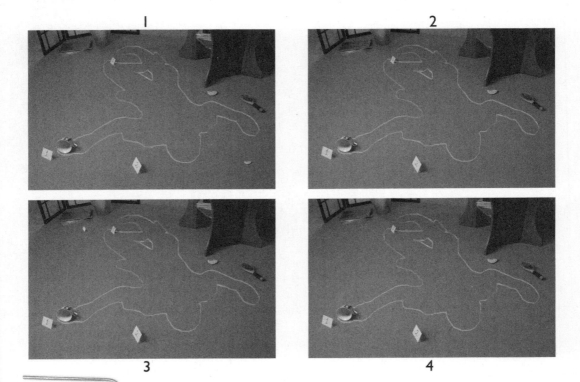

3

4

Answers on page 179.

COLD CASES

The First Instance

Below is a group of words that, when properly arranged in the blanks, reveal a quote from Hannah Arendt.

emergence first have punishment reappearance specific

Whatever the _PUN_____, once a _SPECI____ crime has appeared for the _FIRST_ time, its _____ is more likely than its initial _EMERGEN__ could _HAVE_____ been.

The Role of the State

Below is a group of words that, when properly arranged in the blanks, reveal a quote from Aristotle.

common crime mere prevention sake state

A _____ is not a _____ society, having a _____ place, established for the _____ of mutual _____ and for the _____ of exchange.

COLD CASES

Wrongs Righted

Cryptograms are messages in substitution code. Break the code to read the message. For example, THE SMART CAT might become FVO QWGDF JGF if **F** is substituted for **T, V** for **H, O** for **E,** and so on.

Irxqghg lq 1992 eb Eduub Vfkhfn dqg Shwhu Qhxihog, wkh Lqqrfhqfh Surmhfw dlpv wr hadplqh rog fdvhv dqg jdwkhu qhz hylghqfh, hvshfldoob GQD hylghqfh, wkdw pljkw harqhudwh shrsoh zkr kdyh ehhq zurqjixoob frqylfwhg ri fulphv. Idovh hbhzlwqhvv dffrxqwv kdyh ohg wr vrph zurqjixo frqylfwlrqv, dorqj zlwk wkh fdvhv ri shrsoh zkr sohdghg jxlowb wr d fulph wkhb kdg qrw frpplwwhg lq rughu wr jduqhu d oljkwhu vhqwhefh. Pruh wkdq 350 shrsoh kdyh ehhq iuhhg rq GQD hylghqfh ehfdxvh ri wkh surmhfw'v grjjhg sxuvxlw ri mxvwlfh. Wkh surmhfw ehjdq dv sduw ri d odz vfkrro'v surmhfw, exw frqwlqxhv wrgdb dv d qrq-surilw rujdqlcdwlrq. Wkrxvdqgv ri sulvrqhuv dvn wkh Lqqrfhqfh Surmhfw wr wdnh wkhlu fdvh; d wkrurxjk uhylhz ri wkh fdvh wdnhv sodfh ehiruh wkh Lqqrfhqfh Surmhfw ehjlqv zrun.

Answers on page 180.

The Case of Elizabeth Short (Part I)

Read this true crime account, and then turn to the next page to test your knowledge.

Elizabeth Short, also known as the Black Dahlia, was murdered in 1947. Like thousands of others, Elizabeth wanted to be a star. Unlike the bevy of blondes who trekked to Hollywood, this 22-year-old beauty from Massachusetts was dark and mysterious. She was last seen alive outside the Biltmore Hotel in Los Angeles on the evening of January 9, 1947.

Short's body was found on a vacant lot in Los Angeles. It had been cut in half at the waist and both parts had been drained of blood and then cleaned. Her body parts appeared to be surgically dissected, and her remains were suggestively posed. Despite receiving a number of false confessions and taunting letters that admonished police to "catch me if you can," the crime remains unsolved.

COLD CASES

The Case of Elizabeth Short (Part II)

(Do not read this until you have read the previous page!)

1. **What state did she come from?**
   A. Nevada
   B. Louisiana
   C. Florida
   D. Massachusetts

2. **How old was Elizabeth Short when she died?**
   A. 22
   B. 18
   C. 28
   D. 21

3. **Where was Elizabeth Short last seen alive?**
   A. Manhattan Beach
   B. The Griffith Observatory
   C. The Chateau Marmont Hotel
   D. The Biltmore Hotel

Answers on page 180.

What Changed? (Part I)

Study this picture of the crime scene for 1 minute, then turn the page.

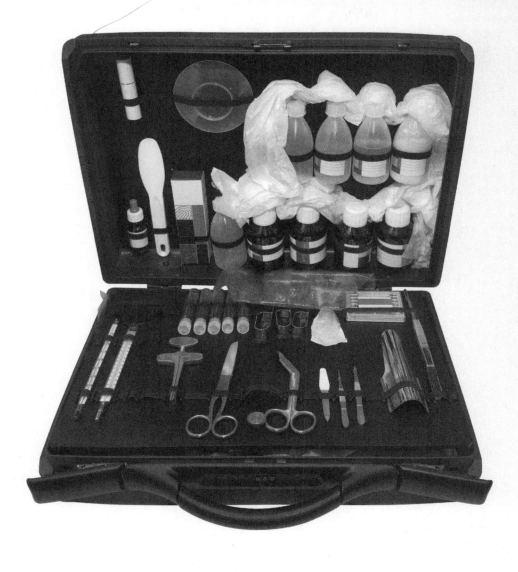

COLD CASES

What Changed? (Part II)

(Do not read this until you have read the previous page!)

From memory, can you tell what changed between this page and the previous page?

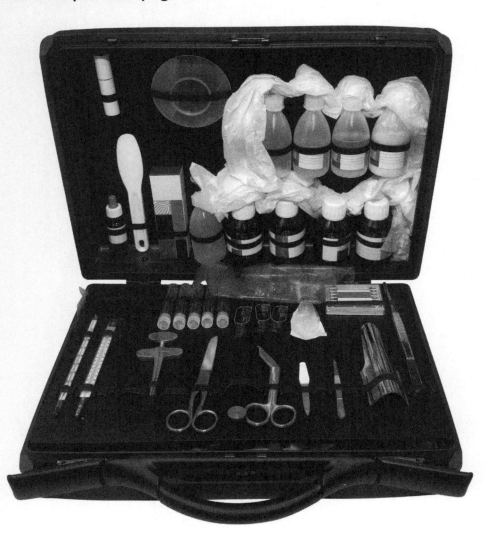

Answers on page 180.

DNA Sequence

Examine the two images below carefully. Are these sequences a match or not?

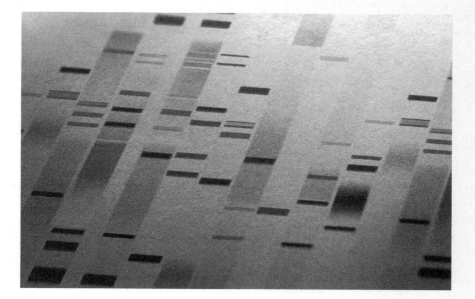

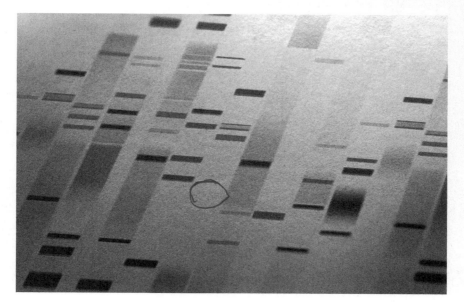

Answers on page 180.

Without a Trace

Cryptograms are messages in substitution code. Break the code to read the message. For example, THE SMART CAT might become FVO QWGDF JGF if **F** is substituted for **T, V** for **H, O** for **E,** and so on.

Usn co jmcgy? Usn co sfcyhn? Usn co oay ksmshimgsf? Byouyyh 1945 shp 1950, xcry kyikfy pcnskkysmyp ch oay smys hysm Byhhchtoih, Rymgiho. S fijsf sqoaim pynjmcbyp co sn oay "Byhhchtoih Omcshtfy." S 74-wysm-ifp aqhoym pcyp uacfy tqcpy s tmiqk ix xyffiu aqhoymn qk s giqhosch, kymaskn sjjcpyhosffw pmiuhyp. Sh 18-wysm-ifp jiffyty noqpyho pcyp uayh nay usn acecht. S ryoymsh pcnskkysmyp xmig s bqn noik sn ay myoqmhyp aigy oi oay Byhhchtoih smys, acn byfihtchtn fyxo byachp ih oay bqn. S jacfp pcnskkysmyp ch 1950 xmig s ryacjfy. Dqno s xyu uyyen sxoym oay biw'n pcnskkysmshjy, s 53-wysm-ifp uigsh pcnskkysmyp uacfy acecht. Aym bipw, qhfcey oaso ix oay ioaymn, usn yryhoqsffw xiqhp.

Answers on page 180.

The Case of Betty Gail Brown (Part I)

Read this true crime account, and then turn to the next page to test your knowledge.

In 1961, a 19-year-old student at Transylvania College who went to a study session never made it home. Betty Gail Brown was found in her car, dead from strangulation. Her own bra had been used as the murder weapon. She hadn't been robbed; her purse and books were left behind. A man named Alex Arnold confessed to the murder in 1965. However, he recanted his confession during trial, and the trial ended in a hung jury. Arnold died in 1980 of cirrhosis of the liver.

The case rocked Lexington, Kentucky, with theories abounding. In 2006, police followed up on one possible lead, a man who had been charged in four strangulations that took place in California. However, that man's prints were not a match for the prints found in Brown's car.

COLD CASES

The Case of Betty Gail Brown (Part II)

(Do not read this until you have read the previous page!)

1. What was the name of Betty Gail Brown's college?

   A. Transylvania College

   B. University of Kentucky

   C. Lexington College

   D. Transvylania University

2. How old was Brown?

   A. 18

   B. 19

   C. 20

   D. 21

3. Alex Arnold confessed in this year.

   A. 1961

   B. 1965

   C. 1980

   D. 2006

Answers on page 180.

COLD CASES

The Suspect's Escape Route

You are standing at a crime scene in a building with only one exit. Elevators are local or express only; there are no stairs. What path did the suspect take to leave the building?

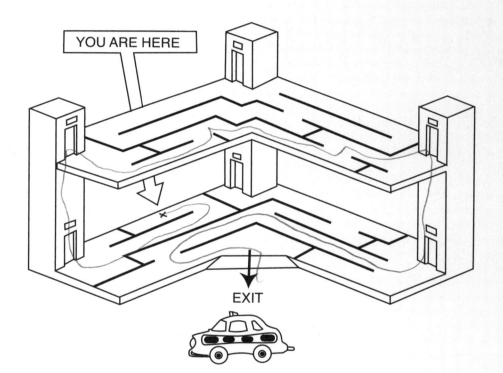

Find a Body

Change just one letter on each line to go from the top word to the bottom word. Do not change the order of the letters. You must have a common English word at each step.

FIND

<u>BIND</u>

<u>BOND</u>

<u>BONY</u>

BODY

Get a Lead in the Case

Change just one letter on each line to go from the top word to the bottom word. Do not change the order of the letters. You must have a common English word at each step.

LEAD

_____

_____

_____

_____

CASE

Answers on page 181.

What Changed? (Part I)

Study this picture for 1 minute, then turn the page.

What Changed? (Part II)

(Do not read this until you have read the previous page!)

From memory, can you tell what changed between this page and the previous page?

Answers on page 181.

Crime Anagrams

Unscramble each word or phrase below to reveal a word or phrase having to do with crime.

SAY SNAIL

BRIEF

NO TABLOIDS

Crime Anagrams

Unscramble each word or phrase below to reveal a word or phrase having to do with crime.

TIP LINE

TIN PILE

DRAWER

SET WINS

COLD CASES

The Jewel Thief's Shopping List

Every gem and term listed below is contained within this group of letters. Complete the word search below to reveal a hidden message related to the puzzle's topic. Words can be found in a straight line horizontally, vertically, or diagonally. They may read either forward or backward.

AGATE   KUNZITE

AMETHYST   ONYX

CARNELIAN   OPAL

CAT'S-EYE   PERIDOT

CHALCEDONY   RUBY

EMERALD   SARD

GARNET   TOPAZ

JADE   ZIRCON

JARGON

Hidden message _____

_____

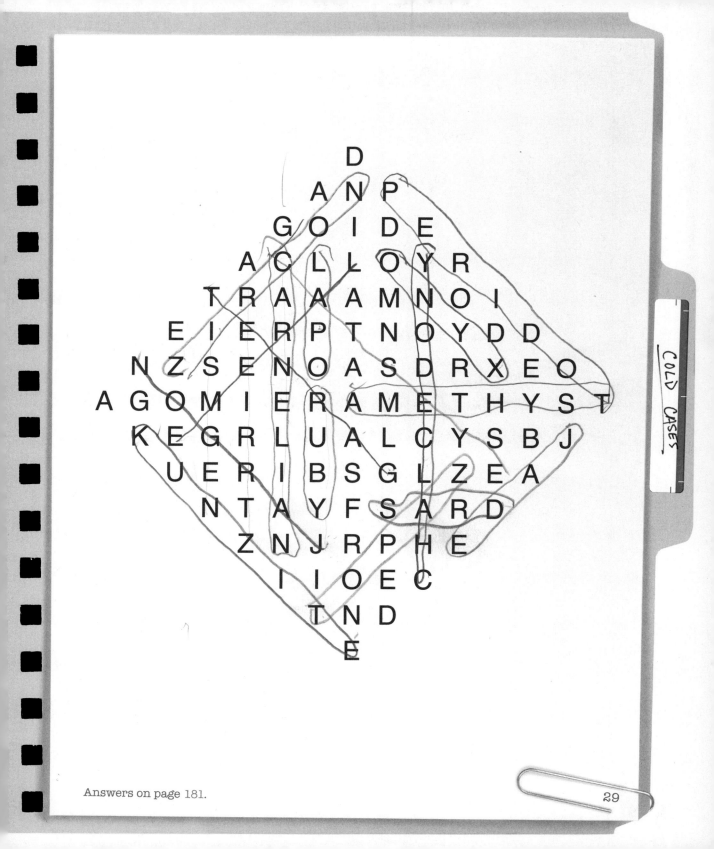

DNA Sequence

Examine the two images below carefully. Are these sequences a match or not?

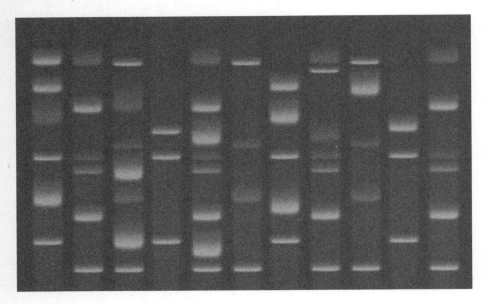

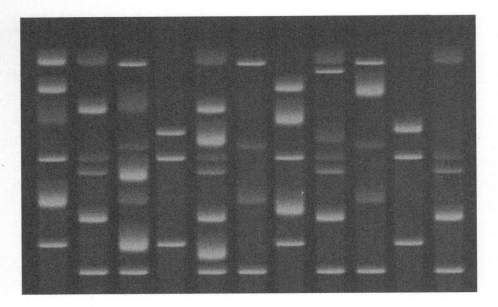

Answers on page 181.

Killing in Depression-Era Cleveland (Part I)

Read this true crime account, and then turn to the next page to test your knowledge.

From 1935 until 1938, a brutal madman roamed the Flats of Cleveland. Despite a massive manhunt, the murderer was never apprehended. In 1935, the Depression had hit Cleveland hard, leaving large numbers of people homeless. Shantytowns sprang up on the eastern side of the city in Kingsbury Run—a popular place for transients.

It is unclear who the first victim was. It may have been an unidentified woman found floating in Lake Erie—in pieces—on September 5, 1934. The first official victim was found in the Jackass Hill area of Kingsbury Run on September 23, 1935. The unidentified body had been dead for almost a month. A mere 30 feet away from the body was another victim, Edward Andrassy. Andrassy had only been dead for days, indicating that the spot was a dumping ground. Police began staking out the area.

After a few months passed without another body, police thought the worst was over. Then on January 26, 1936, the partial remains of a new victim, a woman, were found in downtown Cleveland. On February 7, more remains were found at a separate location, and the deceased was identified as Florence Genevieve Polillo. Despite similarities among the three murders, authorities had yet to connect them—serial killers were highly uncommon at the time.

On June 5, two young boys passing through Kingsbury Run discovered a severed head. The rest of the body was found near the Nickel Plate railroad police station. At this point, Cleveland's newly appointed director of public safety, Eliot Ness, was officially briefed on the case. While Ness and his men hunted down leads, the headless body of another unidentified male was found on July 22, 1936. It appeared that the man had been murdered several months earlier. On September 10, the headless body of a sixth victim was found in Kingsbury Run.

A woman's mutilated torso washed up on a beach on February 23, 1937. The rest would wash ashore two months later. On June 6, 1937, teenager Russell Lauyer found the decomposed body of a woman inside of a burlap sack under the Lorain-Carnegie Bridge in Cleveland. Pieces of another man's body (the ninth victim) began washing ashore on July 6, just below Kingsbury Run.

The next nine months were quiet, and the public began to relax. When a woman's severed leg was found in the Cuyahoga River on April 8, 1938, however, people debated its connection to the Butcher. But the rest of Jane Doe III was soon found inside two burlap sacks floating in the river (sans head, of course).

On August 16, 1938, the last two confirmed victims of the Butcher were found together at the East 9th Street Lakeshore Dump.

Something snapped inside Eliot Ness. On the night of August 18, Ness and dozens of police officials raided the shantytowns in the Flats, ending up in Kingsbury Run. Along the way, they interrogated or arrested anyone they came across, and Ness ordered the shanties burned to the ground. There would be no more confirmed victims of the Mad Butcher of Kingsbury Run.

There were two prime suspects in the case, though no one was ever charged. The first was Dr. Francis Sweeney, a surgeon. (He was also a cousin of Congressman Martin L. Sweeney, a known political opponent of Ness.) In August 1938, Dr. Sweeney was interrogated by Ness, two other men, and the inventor of the polygraph machine, Dr. Royal Grossman. By all accounts, Sweeney failed the polygraph test, and Ness believed he had his man, but he was released due to lack of evidence. Two days after the interrogation, on August 25, 1938, Sweeney checked himself into the Sandusky Veterans Hospital. He remained institutionalized at various facilities until his death in 1965.

The other suspect was Frank Dolezal, who was arrested by private investigators on July 5, 1939, as a suspect in the murder of Florence Polillo, with whom he had lived for a time. While in custody, Dolezal confessed to killing Polillo, although some believe the confession was forced. Either way, Dolezal died under mysterious circumstances while incarcerated at the Cuyahoga County Jail before he could be charged.

COLD CASES

Killing in Depression-Era Cleveland (Part II)

(Do not read this until you have read the previous page!)

1. **True or False:** Eliot Ness will be remembered by history for bringing Cleveland's Torso Killer to justice in 1940.

2. Eliot Ness held this position while investigating the case.
   - A. Sheriff of Cuyahoga County
   - B. Investigator for Cleveland Police
   - C. Private investigator
   - D. Cleveland's director of public safety

3. The bodies were generally left in this Cleveland neighborhood.
   - A. East Cleveland
   - B. Kingsbury's Run
   - C. Slavic Village
   - D. Old City

Answers on page 181.

What Changed? (Part I)

Study this picture of the crime scene for 1 minute, then turn the page.

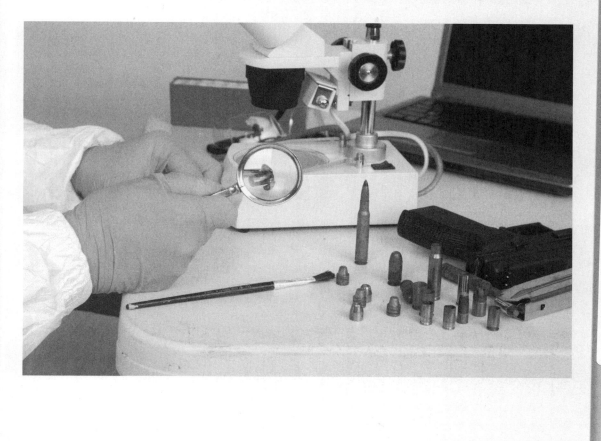

COLD CASES

What Changed? (Part II)

(Do not read this until you have read the previous page!)

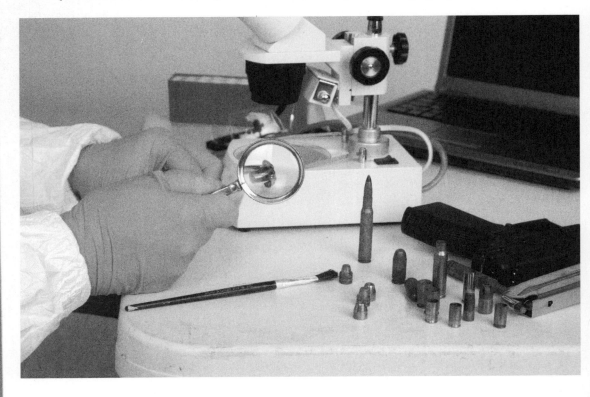

Answers on page 181.

Genetic Fingerprints (Part I)

Read this account, and then turn to the next page to test your knowledge.

It was an unremarkable Monday morning on September 10, 1984. Alec John Jeffreys, now Professor Sir Alec John Jeffreys, was checking the results of some research he was conducting at the University of Leicester. What he saw changed forensics forever: a genetic fingerprint.

The same, complete genetic code is present throughout an entire organism, from a drop of blood to the tip of an eyelash. Before 1984, no one knew how to read that code. One challenge facing scientists was that there is very little genetic difference among members of the same species.

Jeffreys got around this issue by focusing on minisatellites, short bits of the DNA strand that contain a uniquely dense collection of variations. By finding these minisatellites and creating an X-ray image of them, Jeffreys could produce a literal picture of what one made one individual's DNA different from everyone else's.

Within a year of Jeffrey's discovery, genetic fingerprinting was used to save a young boy stuck in an immigration dispute. By 1988, the process had helped convict a murderer. The technology quickly evolved and became a cornerstone to everything from paternity disputes and criminal cases to biological and conservation studies.

COLD CASES

Genetic Fingerprints (Part II)

(Do not read this until you have read the previous page!)

1. The first case to use genetic fingerprinting involved:
    A. A murder investigation
    B. An immigration dispute ✓
    C. An armed robbery
    D. A paternity lawsuit

2. What are minisatellites?
    A. Small, man-made objects that orbit Earth
    B. The section of DNA that all members of a species share ✓
    C. An x-ray image
    D. Small sections of DNA that contain a large number of variations

3. Sir Alec John Jeffreys discovered how to create a genetic fingerprint on:
    A. A Monday morning ✓
    B. A Tuesday afternoon
    C. A Friday morning
    D. A Saturday evening

Answers on page 181.

COLD CASES

DNA Sequence

Examine the two images below carefully. Are these sequences a match or not?

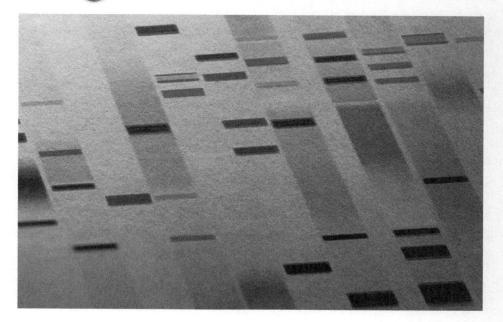

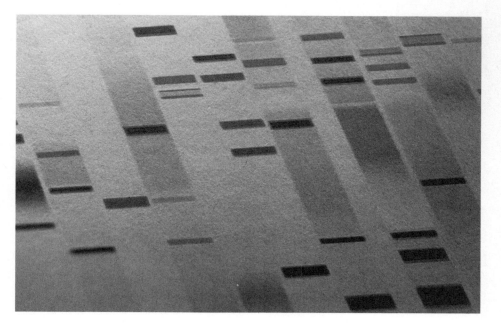

A Famous Disappearance

This cryptogram is encoded using a type of substitution cipher called a Caesar shift. Each letter of the alphabet is replaced by another letter that is a fixed number of positions down the alphabet. For example, THE SMART CAT might become WKH VPDUW FDW with a Caesar shift of 3, where T becomes W, C becomes F, and so forth. With a Caesar shift of 4, it would become XLI WQEVX GEX

Lq 1975, oderu ohdghu Mlppb Kriid glvdsshduhg rq klv zdb wr d Ghwurlw-duhd uhvwdxudqw. Kriid zdv wkh suhvlghqw ri wkh Whdpvwhuv Xqlrq gxulqj wkh 1950v dqg 1960v. Lq 1964, kh zhqw wr mdlo iru eulelqj d judqg mxuru lqyhvwljdwlqj fruuxswlrq lq wkh xqlrq. Lq 1971, kh zdv uhohdvhg rq wkh frqglwlrq wkdw kh qrw sduwlflsdwh lq dqb ixuwkhu xqlrq dfwlylwb. Kriid zdv suhsdulqj d ohjdo fkdoohqjh wr wkdw lqmxqfwlrq zkhq kh glvdsshduhg rq Mxob 30, 1975. Kh zdv odvw vhhq lq wkh sdunlqj orw ri wkh Pdfkxv Uhg Ira Uhvwdxudqw.

Kriid kdg vwurqj frqqhfwlrqv wr wkh Pdild, dqg vhyhudo prevwhuv kdyh fodlphg wkdw kh phw d julvob hqg rq wkhlu vdb vr. Dowkrxjk klv ergb kdv qhyhu ehhq irxqg, dxwkrulwlhv riilfldoob ghfoduhg klp ghdg rq Mxob 30, 1982. Dv uhfhqwob dv Qryhpehu 2006, wkh IEL gxj xs idupodqg lq Plfkljdq krslqj wr wxuq xs d frusvh. Vr idu, qr oxfn.

Answers on page 182.

The Case of Carolyn Wasilewski (Part I)

Read this true crime account, and then turn to the next page to test your knowledge.

The movie 1990 "Cry-Baby," starring Johnny Depp as the leader of a gang of "drapes" in Maryland, evokes a certain rebellious youth subculture of the 1950s. The director, John Waters, was fascinated by stories of drape subculture in his youth, and remembered reading headlines about the November 1954 murder of Carolyn Wasilewski, a 14-year-old "drapette." On the night she died, Wasilewski was meant to meet a friend. She never made it there. Her body was found the following morning, left on a set of railroad tracks. Some of her clothes were missing, and the name "Paul" was written on her thigh. Police concluded that the murder had taken place in a vacant lot near her home before her body was taken to the railyard.

The case set off manhunts and attracted national attention, but remains unsolved and open.

The Case of Carolyn Wasilewski (Part II)

(Do not read this until you have read the previous page!)

1. Carolyn Wasilewski was murdered at a railyard.

True

False ✓

2. The name "Paul" was written on Wasilewski's arm.

True

False ✓

3. The murder took place in November.

True ✓

False

Answers on page 182.

What Changed? (Part I)

Study this picture for 1 minute, then turn the page.

COLD CASES

What Changed? (Part II)

(Do not read this until you have read the previous page!)

From memory, can you tell what changed between this page and the previous page?

Answers on page 182.

Seen at the Scene (Part I)

Study this picture of the crime scene for 1 minute, then turn the page.

COLD CASES

Seen at the Scene (Part II)

(Do not read this until you have read the previous page!)

Which image exactly matches the picture from the previous page?

1

2

3

4

Answers on page 182.

Find the Witness

You want to interview a witness in a cold case, Ken Rawlins. He and his wife have moved since the case was active. From their fomer neighbor, you know they now live on Perkins Avenue, which has five houses, but you don't know which house they live in. They do not have any children. The staff at the bakery around the corner and your own observations give you some clues. From the information given, can you find the right house?

1. **There are married couples in two of the houses.**
2. **Kids live in the middle house and one of the houses next door.**
3. **An elderly widower lives in one of the corner houses.**
4. **A single mom with custody of her kids lives in house D.**
5. **A widow lives next door to the widower and they have recently begun dating.**

House A   House B   House C   House D   House E

Answers on page 182.

Don't Miss a Clue

Change just one letter on each line to go from the top word to the bottom word. Do not change the order of the letters. You must have a common English word at each step.

MISS

_____

_____

_____

_____

_____

_____

_____

CLUE

Answers on page 182.

Mayhem on Wall Street (Part I)

Read this account, and then turn to the next page to test your knowledge.

Noon, September 16, 1920. Workers on their lunch breaks were leaving offices on the corner of Wall and Broad streets, the heart of New York City's financial district. A man pulled up in a horse-drawn wagon, jumped down, and left. Seconds later, the wagon—packed with dynamite—exploded, killing 38 people and injuring more than 300.

The next day, postal workers found flyers that had been left in the area the day before the attack. The flyers asked for the release of unspecified political prisoners and were signed, "American Anarchist Fighters." The flyers and the style of the bomb were similar to ones used in previous anarchist attacks. But officials could not glean much more information than that.

Most of the suspects investigated were known Italian anarchists such as Pietro Angelo and Luigi Galleani. But Angelo had an alibi, and Galleani had been in Italy, deported for his involvement in a 1919 bombing.

Ultimately, officials could not tie the bombing to anyone. The case officially closed in 1940. In 1944, the FBI briefly reopened it and decided the attack was probably done by unknown Italian anarchists or terrorists. Who specifically perpetrated the crime, however, remains unknown.

COLD CASES

Mayhem on Wall Street (Part II)

(Do not read this until you have read the previous page!)

1. The flyers left in the area the day before the bombing asked for:
    A. An end to capitalism in the United States
    B. The pardon of Luigi Galleani
    C. A military alliance with Italy
    D. The release of political prisoners

2. The Wall Street bombing took place at:
    A. Midnight
    B. 5:00 p.m.
    C. Noon
    D. 8:00 a.m.

3. How was the bomb transported to the site?
    A. In a horse-drawn wagon
    B. Carried by a pedestrian
    C. In an automobile
    D. Authorities do not know for sure.

Answers on page 182.

DNA Sequence

Examine the two images below carefully. Are these sequences a match or not?

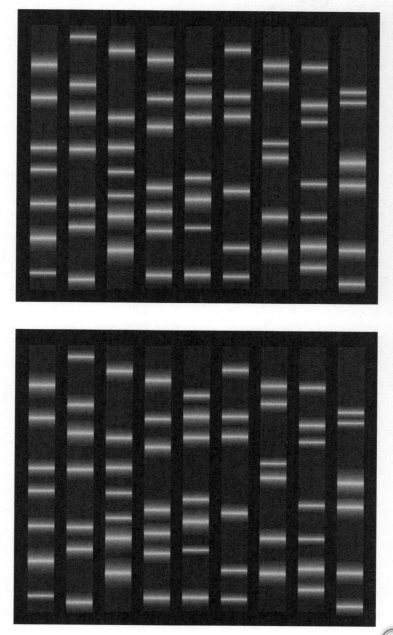

Answers on page 182.

The Suspect's Escape Route

You are standing at a crime scene in a building with only one exit. Elevators are local or express only; there are no stairs. What path did the suspect take to leave the building?

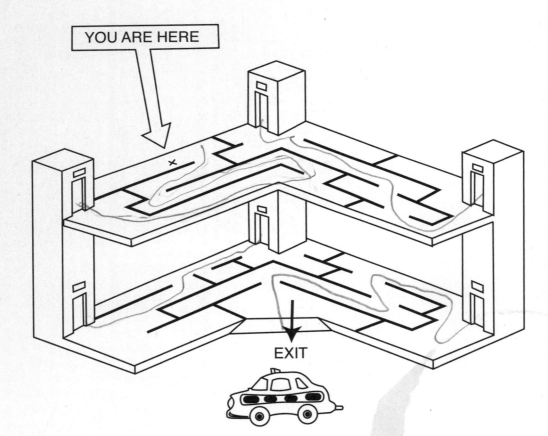

YOU ARE HERE

EXIT

Answers on page 182.

What Changed? (Part I)

Study this picture for 1 minute, then turn the page.

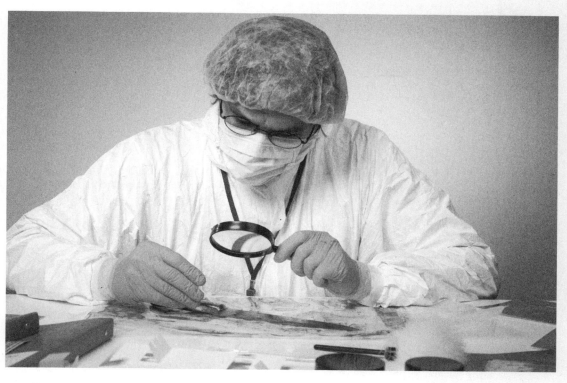

BISSEL
9:45

COLD CASES

What Changed? (Part II)

(Do not read this until you have read the previous page!)

From memory, can you tell what changed between this page and the previous page?

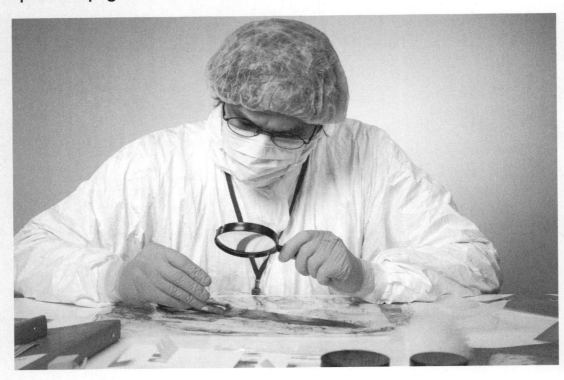

Answers on page 182.

Crime Anagrams

Unscramble each word or phrase below to reveal a word or phrase having to do with crime.

MIDI ECHO
TATER BY
NAPE OW

Virgil on Crime

Below is a group of words that, when properly arranged in the blanks, reveal a quote from Virgil.

brass forms name punishment tell thousand voice

Had I a _Thou_ tongues, a hundred mouths, a _voice_ of iron and a chest of _BRASS_, I could not _Tell_ all the _Forms_ of crime, could not _Name_ all the types of _Punis_.

COLD CASES

DNA Sequence

Examine the two images below carefully. Are these sequences a match or not?

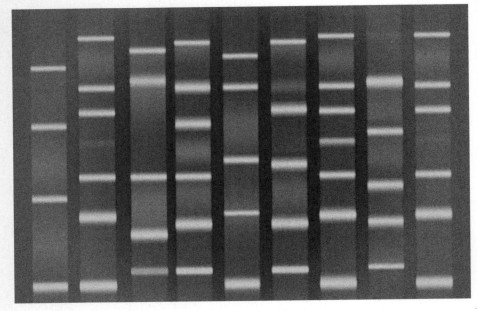

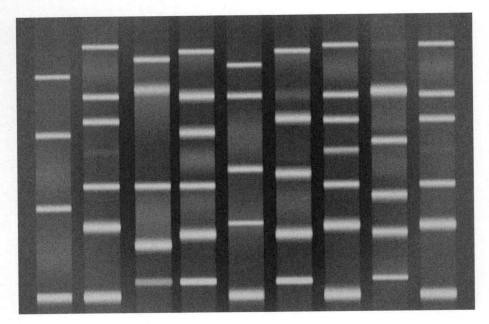

Answers on page 183.

The Connecticut River Valley Killer (Part I)

Read this true crime account, and then turn to the next page to test your knowledge.

The murders attributed to the serial killer nicknamed the Connecticut River Valley Killer between 1978 and 1987 did not actually take place in Connecticut, but in New Hampshire and Vermont. (The Connecticut River flows through Massachusetts, Vermont, and New Hampshire in addition to Connecticut.)

The assumed first victim, Cathy Millican, died in 1978. Her body was found at the New Hampshire wetland preserve where she had been photographing birds. She had been stabbed about 30 times. The body of a second woman was found in 1981. At the time, police did not connect the two cases. Then, in the mid-1980s, three women disappeared. The condition of their bodies when they were found pointed towards stab wounds. Looking back at previous cases, investigators began to establish connections that pointed to a serial killer. At least seven women were believed to have been killed.

In 1988, a woman named Jane Boroski stopped at a convenience store in New Hampshire, where she was approached by the driver of the vehicle next to hers. He dragged her from her car and stabbed her repeatedly before driving away. Amazingly, Boroski managed to get back in her car and reach her friend's home, even though she saw her assilant's car on the road. While Boroski was able to work with the police to provide a composite sketch of her assailant, he was never found. No further murders happened, and the case went cold.

The Connecticut River Valley Killer (Part II)

(Do not read this until you have read the previous page!)

1. The body of the first presumed victim was found at this location.
    A. Convenience store
    B. Her home
    C. A wetland preserve ✓
    D. A forest

2. About this many murders are attributed to the killer.
    A. 3
    B. 5
    (C.) 7
    D. 15

3. Jane Boroski survived an attack from the probable killer in this state.
    A. Vermont
    B. Connecticut
    C. Massachusetts
    (D.) New Hampshire

Answers on page 183.

What Changed? (Part I)

Study this picture for 1 minute, then turn the page.

What Changed? (Part II)

(Do not read this until you have read the previous page!)

From memory, can you tell what changed between this page and the previous page?

Answers on page 183.

Without a Trace

Cryptograms are messages in substitution code. Break the code to read the message. For example, THE SMART CAT might become FVO QWGDF JGF if **F** is substituted for **T, V** for **H, O** for **E,** and so on.

Len chbn Admyk Hybé Hmvmklyc An Fjyczn gdnkc'l bnhc bmze ld bdkl fndfan, uml kdbn unaynon en qhk len pyjkl fnjkdc ld jnzdjg bdoycv ybhvnk dc pyab, h vddg knonc wnhjk unpdjn Ledbhk Ngykdc. Qenlenj dj cdl en gyg kd yk dfnc ld gnuhln, hk yk qehl ehffncng ld eyb dc Knflnbunj 16, 1890. Dc lehl ghw, An Fjyczn'k ujdlenj hzzdbfhcyng eyb ld len ljhyc klhlydc yc Gysdc, Pjhczn, qenjn en qhk kzengmang ld lhtn len nrfjnkk ljhyc ld Fhjyk. Qenc len ljhyc jnhzeng Fhjyk, edqnonj, An Fjyczn hcg eyk amvvhvn qnjn cdqenjn ld un pdmcg. Len ljhyc qhk knhjzeng, hk qnjn len ljhztk unlqnnc Gysdc hcg Fhjyk, uml cd kyvc dp An Fjyczn dj eyk amvvhvn qhk nonj pdmcg. Lendjynk hudml eyk gykhffnhjhczn jhcvn pjdb eyk unycv bmjgnjng pdj ljwycv ld pyvel Ngykdc donj len fhlncl dp len pyjkl bdlydc fyzlmjn ld eyk phbyaw pdjzycv eyb ld vd ycld eygycv ld tnnf eyb khpn pjdb fndfan qed qhclng eyk fhlnclk pdj lenbknaonk. Dlenjk unaynon lehl An Fjyczn lddt eyk dqc aypn unzhmkn en qhk cnhjaw uhctjmfl.

A Motive for Murder

Every word listed is contained within the group of letters. Words can be found in a straight line horizontally, vertically, or diagonally. They may read either forward or backward.

BILL

BITCOIN

BREAD

BUCKS

CAPITAL

CHANGE

CHECK

CHIPS

CURRENCY

DOLLAR

DOUGH

FORTUNE

FUNDS

GOLD

GRAVY

GREEN

LOOT

MINT

MONEY

MULLAH

NOTE

PILE

RICHES

SCRIP

TENDER

TREASURE

WAD

WEALTH

```
H U J K Y K G M H G U O D I E
T R E A S U R E I L C I W N B
L D K A B H S I P N U E U A G
A Q P V W K B V B F T T F C D
E R S I C S P I H C R U A P G
W A V U R C T B O O N P S C T
C L B E T C W I F D I D H H E
E L T R O O S L S T H L A A N
L O V I E H O L A G S O L N D
N D N J I A V L T R E G L G E
N M O N E Y D Y K E H P U E R
P C U R R E N C Y E C Y M M J
F I G K F B E Y H N I G H V Q
T N L Q I H H D Z E R F E F C
G I A E C D V W Y V A R G P G
```

COLD CASES

DNA Sequence

Examine the two images below carefully. Are these sequences a match or not?

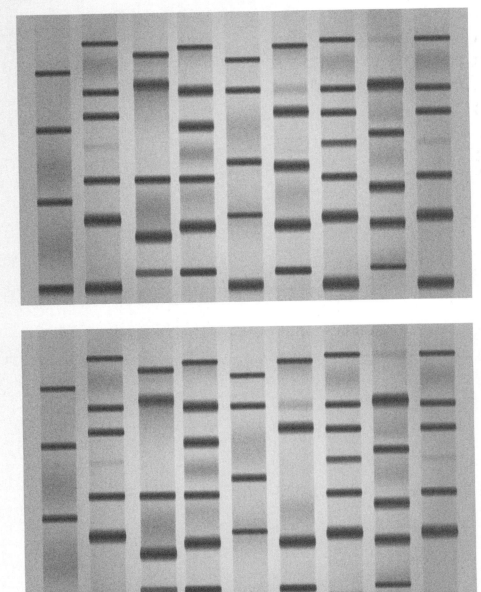

Answers on page 183.

DNA Quiz

How much do you know about DNA?

1. What does DNA stand for?
    A. Deoxyribonucleic acid
    B. Dynamic nucleic acid
    C. Derivative nucleotidic acid
    D. Deoxynucleic acid

2. Cytosine is one of the four bases found in DNA.
   Name the other three.

   _____

   _____

   _____

3. Which statement below is true?
    A. DNA can be gathered from blood, skin, saliva, and hair.
    B. DNA can be gathered from blood, skin, and saliva, but not hair.
    C. DNA can be gathered from blood and hair, but not saliva or skin.

Answers on page 183.

The Cat Burglar

Maurice St. Clair is considered by many to be the most successful cat burglar of the 20th century. As a local crime reporter, you've been given an assignment to write a story about six of his most daring heists spanning more than 30 years. Using only the clues below, match each of these thefts to the correct month, year, and location, and determine what was stolen in each.

1. The 1991 theft (which wasn't in Seattle) was either the one that happened on July 4th or the one involving the collection of rare blue diamonds.

2. The cash heist, the one in 1998, and the one that took place on April 13th were three different events.

3. Maurice's infamous "Halloween heist" (so-called because it happened on October 31st) didn't involve either diamonds or rubies.

4. Of the cash theft and the Vancouver heist, one happened in July and the other occurred in 1984.

5. The Berlin burglary happened 7 years after the Halloween heist.

6. Of Maurice's 1991 burglary and the one that happened in Paris, one involved blue diamonds and the other occurred on June 15th.

7. The September theft happened sometime after Maurice's infamous London heist.

8. The Seattle heist (which didn't happen in the 1980s) didn't take place in July.

9. The Halloween heist happened 7 years before Maurice's September 10th theft (which involved a large number of pure gold bars).

10. The emerald theft happened sometime before the June 15th heist.

11. The July 4th heist occurred 14 years after the sapphire burglary.

	Cities						Items						Months					
	Antwerp	Berlin	London	Paris	Seattle	Vancouver	Cash	Diamonds	Emeralds	Gold bars	Rubies	Sapphires	April	May	June	July	October	September
Years 1963																		
1970																		
1977																		
1984																		
1991																		
1998																		
Months April																		
May																		
June																		
July																		
October																		
September																		
Items Cash																		
Diamonds																		
Emeralds																		
Gold bars																		
Rubies																		
Sapphires																		

Years	Cities	Items	Months
1963			
1970			
1977			
1984			
1991			
1998			

The Suspect's Escape Route

You are standing at a crime scene in a building with only one exit. Elevators are local or express only; there are no stairs. What path did the suspect take to leave the building?

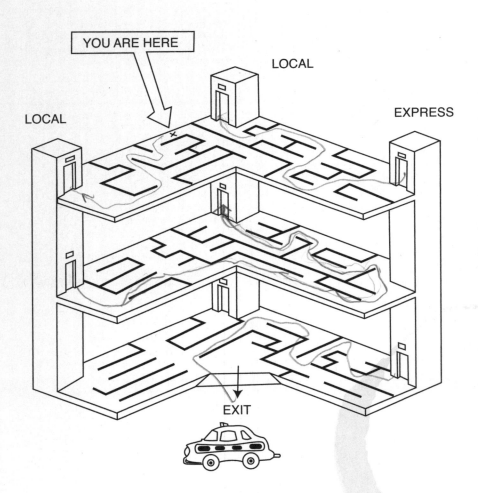

Answers on page 184.

What Changed? (Part I)

Study this picture for 1 minute, then turn the page.

What Changed? (Part II)

(Do not read this until you have read the previous page!)

From memory, can you tell what changed between this page and the previous page?

Answers on page 184.

Will New Clues Lead to
a Break in the Case?

Change just one letter on each line to go from the top word to the bottom word. Do not change the order of the letters. You must have a common English word at each step.

CLUES

_____

_____

_____

_____

(precedes chicken, rice, and green tomatoes)

_____

_____

_____

BREAK

COLD CASES

DNA Sequence

Examine the two images below carefully. Are these sequences a match or not?

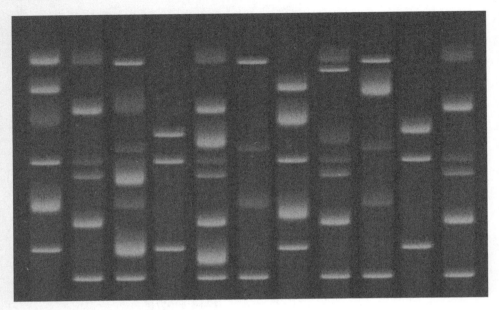

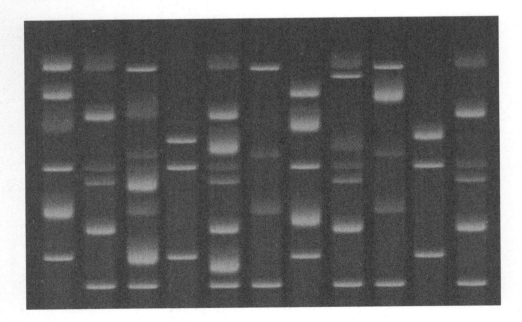

Answers on page 184.

The Great Plains Butcher (Part I)

Read this true crime account, and then turn to the next page to test your knowledge.

In many cold cases, the victims are known while the killer is a cipher. In the case of Eugene Butler, we know he murdered six people and buried them on his property. Their identitites, however, remain unknown.

Eugene Butler died in 1913 in North Dakota State Hospital, an asylum for the mentally ill. He had been admitted there in 1906 after suffering from hallucinations and paranoid delusions. It was not until after his death that the bodies of his victims were found, when workmen sent by his relatives to renovate the property discovered a series of skeletons under the cellar. They were young men, probably itinerant farmhands hired by Butler. Butler killed them by crushing their skulls; he even built a trap door to more easily dispose of the remains. None of the victims have been identified, and some of the bones were even stolen, probably by people looking for grisly souvenirs of a case that captured the public's imagination.

The Great Plains Butcher (Part II)

(Do not read this until you have read the previous page!)

1. Eugene Butler died in this year.
    A. 1906
    B. 1913 ✓
    C. 1912
    D. Unknown

2. The bodies were found by:
    A. Children searching an abandoned property
    B. Butler's relatives come to tour their inheritance
    C. Doctors from the state's asylum
    D. Workmen excavating the property ✓

3. Butler used this method to kill his victims.
    A. Strangulation
    B. Crushing their skulls ✓
    C. Pushing them through a trap door into a pit
    D. Burying them alive

Answers on page 184.

Find the Witness

On Calendar Court, there are 5 houses that are identical to each other. You need to follow up with a witness, Yvette White, but without any address on the doors you are not sure which house to approach. You know that from a previous statement that White and her husband have two children, a boy and a girl. The staff at the corner coffee shop and your own observations give you some clues. From the information given, can you find the right house?

A. One staff member says she knows that the couple in house A do not have children, but every other house has at least one child.

B. Another staff member isn't sure where White lives, but he says he's heard her say that she's lucky that both her next door neighbors have kids for her kids to play with.

C. There's a house with a newborn baby somewhere on the block, but not next door to White.

D. The house with the newborn is not next to the couple without children.

House A   House B   House C   House D   House E

Answers on page 184.

Fingerprint Match

There are 8 sets of fingerprints. Find each match.

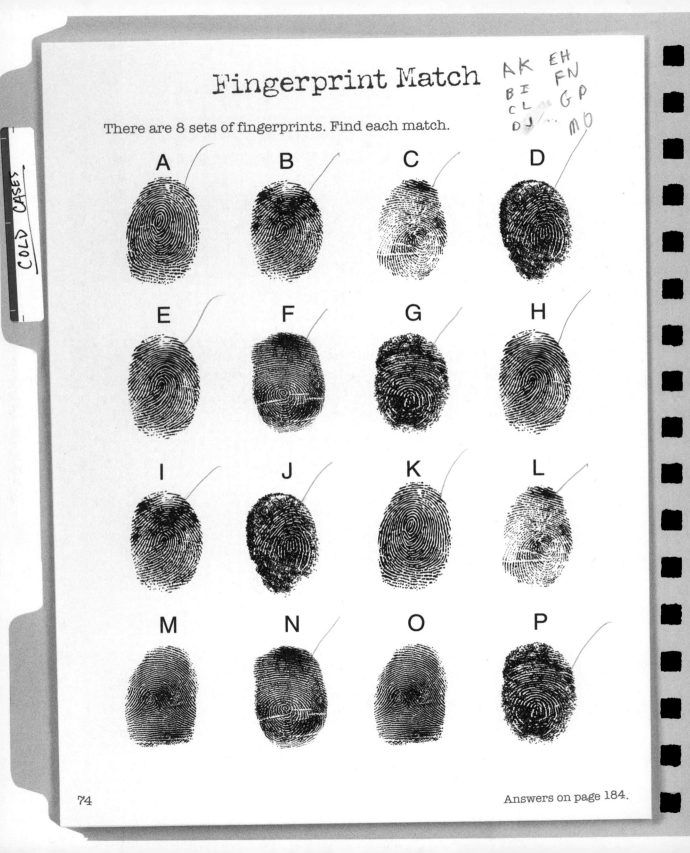

A B C D

E F G H

I J K L

M N O P

74

Answers on page 184.

What Changed? (Part I)

Study this picture for 1 minute, then turn the page.

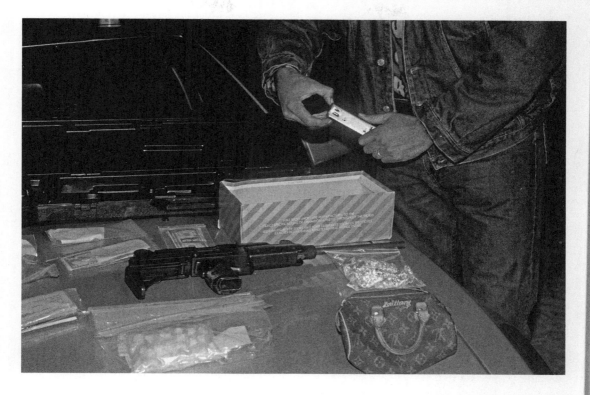

(Do not read this until you have read the previous page!)

From memory, can you tell what changed between this page and the previous page?

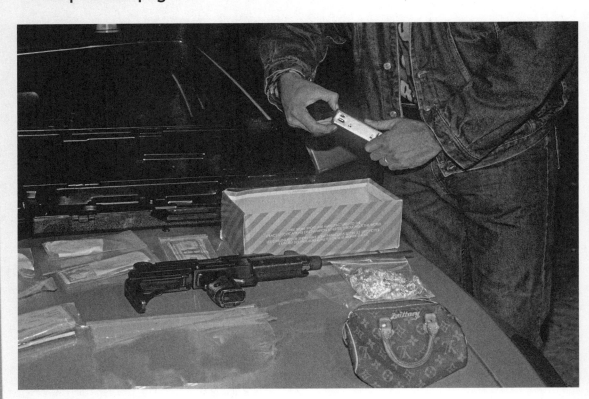

Answers on page 184.

Seen at the Scene (Part I)

Study this picture of the crime scene for 1 minute, then turn the page.

COLD CASES

Seen at the Scene (Part II)

(Do not read this until you have read the previous page!)

Which image exactly matches the picture from the previous page?

1   2

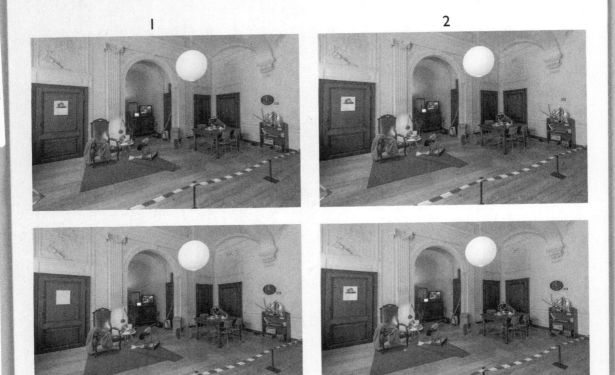

3   4

Answers on page 184.

DNA Sequence

Examine the two images below carefully. Are these sequences a match or not?

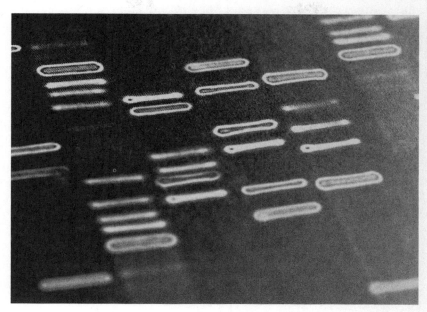

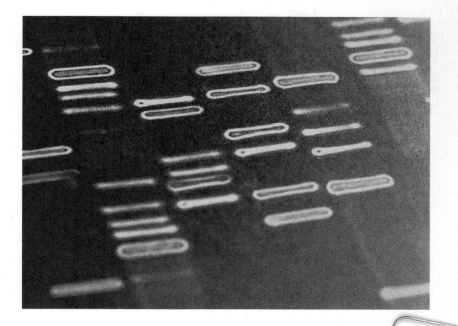

COLD CASES

Unlock the Safe

Crack the code to unlock the safe! The goal of this puzzle is to replace the question marks with a correct sequence of numbers. The numbers you need for the answer are contained in the rows above the question marks. Follow these 2 guides: A black dot indicates that a number needed for the solution is in that row and in the correct position; a white dot means that a number needed for the solution is in that row but in the wrong position. Numbers do not appear more than once in the solution, and the solution never begins with 0.

6 3 2 ○ ○

2 4 8 ○

5 6 0 ○

7 9 1 ●

———————

? ? ?

Answers on page 184.

The Zodiac Killer (Part I)

Read this true crime account, and then turn to the next page to test your knowledge.

The Zodiac Killer was responsible for several murders in the San Francisco area in the 1960s and 1970s. His victims were shot, stabbed, and bludgeoned to death. After the first few kills, he began sending letters to the local press in which he taunted police and made public threats, such as planning to blow up a school bus. In a letter sent to the "San Francisco Chronicle" two days after the murder of cabbie Paul Stine in October 1969, the killer, who called himself "The Zodiac," included in the package pieces of Stine's blood-soaked shirt. In the letters, which continued until 1978, he claimed a cumulative tally of 37 murders.

COLD CASES

The Zodiac Killer (Part II)

(Do not read this until you have read the previous page!)

1. The Zodiac Killer always bludgeoned his victims to death.

True

False ✓

2. The killer sent a letter to this newspaper.

A. San Francisco Chronicle ✓

B. Los Angeles Times

C. New York Times

D. Sacramento Daily News

3. How many murders did the Zodiac Killer Claim?

A. 32

B. 37 ✓

C. 73

Answers on page 184.

COLD CASES

What Changed? (Part I)

Study this picture for 1 minute, then turn the page.

What Changed? (Part II)

(Do not read this until you have read the previous page!)

From memory, can you tell what changed between this page and the previous page?

Answers on page 184.

Dizzier Noble

Unscramble the anagrams below to reveal names and terms associated with the Lizzie Borden case.

CHASMS STATUES (place name)

RAVE FRILL (place name)

WARDEN (personal name of one of the victims)

BARBED BONY (personal name of one of the victims)

DEBT RIG (personal name of the maid)

HAT ETCH (tool)

WACKY FROTHS (term in nursery rhyme)

HOT TEMPERS (family role)

Answers on page 185.

The Suspect's Escape Route

You are standing at a crime scene in a building with only one exit. Elevators are local or express only; there are no stairs. What path did the suspect take to leave the building?

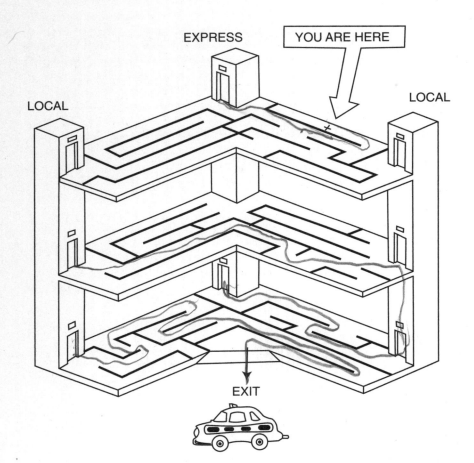

Answers on page 185.

Tracing the Suspect

The suspect visited eight cities. Can you put the list of the eight cities he visited in order, using the information below?

1. The suspect proceeded directly from Maryland to Wisconsin.

2. San Diego was one of the final four cities.

3. Oklahoma City was one of the first four cities.

4. The suspect did not begin his journey in Topeka, Milwaukee, or Boise.

5. The suspect did not end his journey in Charleston, Oklahoma City, or Baltimore.

6. After Milwaukee, he visited exactly two other cities before visiting Atlanta.

7. After Oklahoma City, he visited exactly two other cities before visiting San Diego.

8. South Carolina was visited immediately before Kansas.

9. The city whose name begins with a C was visited before the cities beginning with A or B.

10. The suspect stopped in Idaho sometime after California but before Georgia.

Answers on page 185.

Parallel Words

Of the following words, which is the closest in meaning to "coagulated"?

A. **Rough**
B. **Solid**
C. **Thick**
D. **Synthesized**
E. **Vapid**

Sorry for Their Crimes?

Which word is the odd one out?

repentant

penitent

contrite

remorseful

sympathetic

Answers on page 185.

COLD CASES

DNA Sequence

Examine the two images below carefully.
Are these sequences a match or not?

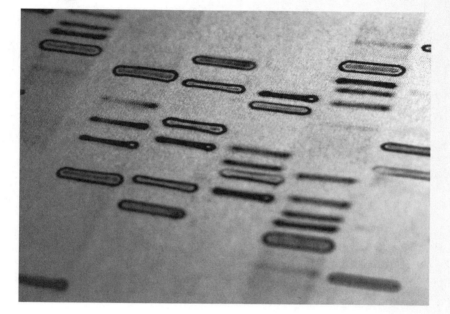

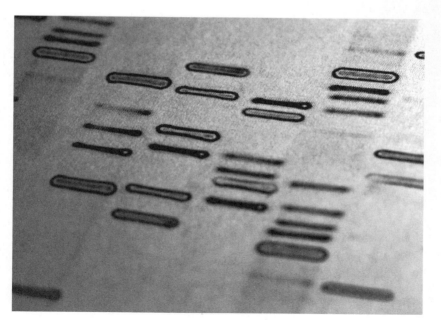

Answers on page 185.

COLD CASES

An Effective Deterrence?

Below is a group of words that, when properly arranged in the blanks, reveal a quote from Mary Wollstonecraft.

anyone commission committing death fear never present

The _____ of ignominious _____, I believe, _____ deterred _____ from the _____ of a crime, because in _____ it the mind is roused to activity about _____ circumstances.

From the Aeneid

Below is a group of words that, when properly arranged in the blanks, reveal a quote from Virgil.

crime from know nation single

_____ a _____ _____ _____ the _____.

Answers on page 185.

COLD CASES

What Changed? (Part I)

Study this picture for 1 minute, then turn the page.

What Changed? (Part II)

(Do not read this until you have read the previous page!)

From memory, can you tell what changed between this page and the previous page?

Answers on page 185.

Seen at the Scene (Part I)

Study this picture of the crime scene for 1 minute, then turn the page.

Seen at the Scene (Part II)

(Do not read this until you have read the previous page!)

Which image exactly matches the crime scene?

1

2

3

4

Answers on page 185.

DNA Sequence

Examine the two images below carefully. Are these sequences a match or not?

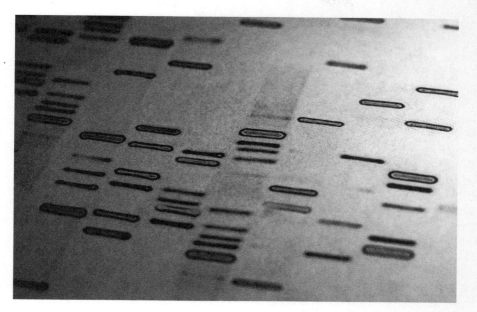

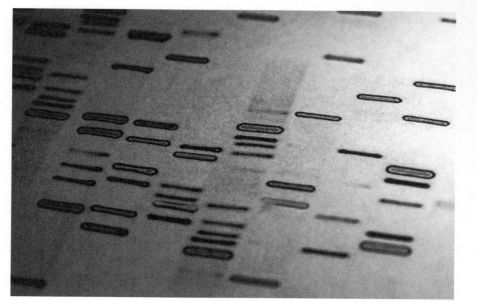

A Murder in Vegas

Every word listed is contained within the group of letters. Words can be found in a straight line horizontally, vertically, or diagonally. They may be read either forward or backward.

ANTE	JEOPARDY
BAD LUCK	ODDS
BET	RISK
CALCULATION	SPECULATION
CHANCE	TEMPT FORTUNE
DANGER	TOSS UP
GAMBLE	UNCERTAINTY
GOOD LUCK	VENTURE
HAZARD	WAGER

```
J K D Y E W L B K C U L D O O G A
S Q H A Z A R D K W D I V V B E U
J Y A P A S B A M N D M E T S T Y
B E Z A J A Z Y D A N O N S D N R
E L L S D K X U Z O S D T B E A X
T Y E L L Y E G I P K D U X P H D
P O U Z T D A T E P C S R P P N J
H C S J M M A C E B U H E E D X S
K D C S B L U N C E R T A I N T Y
G V J L U L Z W K T N G J N T V T
O O E C A P F I T P X E G I C N E
Y U L T T E M P T F O R T U N E B
O A I R S U X N W P T V E H F W C
C O Z T R Z U K A G J K O G A L T
N L D A N G E R Z B J S J G D A S
P J H C E A D S B C X I E K S C K
I O G I A Y B M Q G G R A M A E J
```

A Disappearance in 1910

Cryptograms are messages in substitution code. Break the code to read the message. For example, THE SMART CAT might become FVO QWGDF JGF if **F** is substituted for **T, V** for **H, O** for **E,** and so on.

Kypsm ojsghbgn fiop iy Hsqsfzsm 12, 1910, oaijjbgn bg Fkgakppkg, Kfsmbqkg oiqbkebps Himipaw Kmgieh pieh k ymbsgh oas uko jekggbgn pi uked aifs pamirna Qsgpmke Jkmd. Oas gstsm fkhs bp. Yskmbgn pasbm hkrnapsm akh seijsh ubpa asm igs-pbfs ziwymbsgh Nsimns Nmboqif, Cm., pas Kmgieho bffshbkpsew abmsh pas Jbgdsmpig Hspsqpbts Knsgqw, kepairna pasw hbh gip msjimp asm fboobgn pi jiebqs rgpbe kefiop k figpa ekpsm. Igqs pas jmsoo askmh pas gsuo, pasimbso ojmskh ebds ubehybms, fiop iy pasf jibgpbgn pas ybgnsm kp Nmboqif. Oifs zsebstsh as akh frmhsmsh Kmgieh, zrp ipasmo pairnap oas akh hbsh ko pas msorep iy k zipqash kzimpbig. Opbee ipasmo ysep asm ykfbew akh zkgboash asm pi Oubpxsmekgh kgh pasg rosh asm hbokjjskmkgqs ko k qitsm-rj. Gi stbhsgqs uko stsm yirgh pi yimfkeew qakmns Nmboqif, kgh Kmgieh'o hbokjjskmkgqs msfkbgo rgoietsh.

Answers on page 186.

What Changed? (Part I)

Study this picture for 1 minute, then turn the page.

What Changed? (Part II)

(Do not read this until you have read the previous page!)

From memory, can you tell what changed between this page and the previous page?

CRIME INVESTIGATION

FORENSIC LABORATORY

Answers on page 186.

DNA Sequence

Examine the two images below carefully. Are these sequences a match or not?

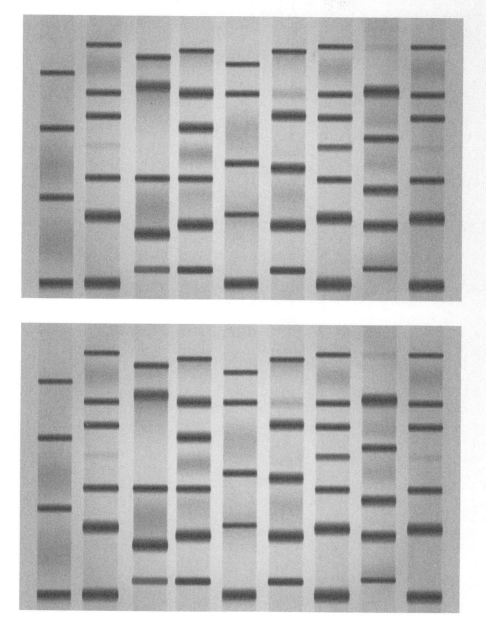

The Suspect's Escape Route

You are standing at a crime scene in a building with only one exit. Elevators are local or express only; there are no stairs. What path did the suspect take to leave the building?

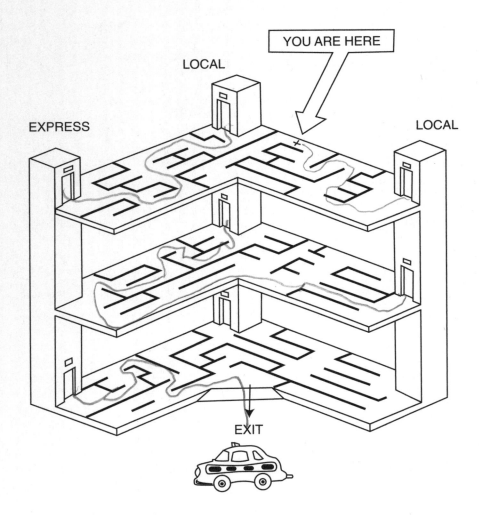

Answers on page 186.

Seen at the Scene (Part I)

Study this picture of the crime scene for 1 minute, then turn the page.

Seen at the Scene (Part II)

(Do not read this until you have read the previous page!)

Which image exactly matches the picture from the previous page?

1

2

3

4

Answers on page 186.

COLD CASES

Jar Etch Kipper

Unscramble the anagrams below to reveal names and terms associated with Jack the Ripper, perhaps the most famous cold case of them all.

ETHICAL PHEW (place name)

DASTARDLY CON (headquarters)

STOUTER PITS (the victims were these)

GORIER POLYP (the study of the case)

ELEPHANT ROAR (a nickname for the killer)

SAD TEEN (place name)

FINANCIAL COVE (term for the known victims)

BAD ROSES (message allegedly written by the killer)

SAC JAY YUCK (message allegedly written by the killer)

OH MR FELL (message allegedly written by the killer)

GOUGERS ELK (head of the Whitechapel Vigilance Committee; recipient of one of the letters above)

COLD CASES

The Poison Was Found in the...

Every word listed is contained within the group of letters. Words can be found in a straight line horizontally, vertically, or diagonally. They may read either forward or backward.

ANGEL FOOD

BABKA

BAKED ALASKA

BAKLAVA

BERRY

BLINI

BROWNIE

CHAPATI

COCOA

COMPOTE

COOKIE

CREPE

CRULLER

CUPCAKE

FLAN

FONDUE

GATEAU

GINGERBREAD

ICING

MOCHA

MOUSSE

NOUGAT

PASTRY

PEACH MELBA

PROFITEROLE

SWISS ROLL

TIRAMISU

TORTE

TRIFLE

TUTTI-FRUTTI

WHIPPED CREAM

ZABAGLIONE

```
V X R A X D U D D F O N D U E
C W W B O K W O U C I T E F S
X H O D M C O M P O T E A T F
I S A W R F O C M O U S S E O
C V B P L J R C D K M M K S T
I Z Q E A U B U S I M A R I T
N D G N L T L Q C E G E E E I
G N O L D C I C V X I R Q E T
A P E N I J N F E K A C P U C
T R R K T O I E P Y N D A F E
E O F A U T T E E T Z E K P J
A F O G D R B E R R Y P S N W
U I A O O R D I C C V P A H W
X T U T T I F R U T T I L R N
L E N O I L G A B A Z H A U M
B R L T E Y R T S A P W D C O
F O E J E I N W O R B F E F C
L L O R S S I W S J D K K P H
P E A C H M E L B A K L A V A
N G I N G E R B R E A D B C F
```

DNA Sequence

Examine the two images below carefully. Are these sequences a match or not?

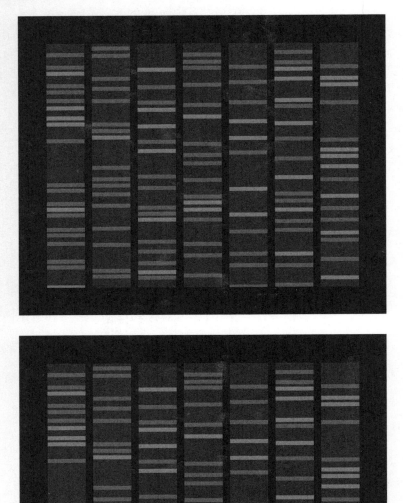

Answers on page 187.

A Murder in Sweden (Part I)

Read this true crime account, and then turn to the next page to test your knowledge.

On February 28, 1986, Swedish Prime Minister Olof Palme was gunned down on a Stockholm street as he and his wife strolled home from the movies unprotected around midnight. The prime minister was fatally shot in the back. His wife was seriously wounded but survived.

In 1988, a petty thief and drug addict named Christer Pettersson was convicted of the murder because he was picked out of a lineup by Palme's widow. The conviction was later overturned on appeal when doubts were raised as to the reliability of Mrs. Palme's evidence. Despite many theories, the assassin remains at large. As a politician, Palme had made enemies, and some speculated he was assassinated by pro-apartheid South African forces, as he was anti-apartheid; by right-wing Chilean fascists for his support of Chilean leftists; or even by extremist Swedish police forces.

COLD CASES

A Murder in Sweden (Part II)

(Do not read this until you have read the previous page!)

1. Olof Palme was killed going home from an outing to:
   A. A diplomatic dinner
   B. The movies
   C. The opera
   D. A shopping mall

2. The prime suspect was named:
   A. Chris Peterson
   B. Christer Pettersson
   C. Cristof Patterson
   D. Kris Petersen

3. The main evidence against the suspect was:
   A. His prints were found on the gun
   B. He confessed to the crime
   C. Palme's widow picked him out of a lineup
   D. He was named in a tip line

Answers on page 187.

A Quip from Seneca

Below is a group of words that, when properly arranged in the blanks, reveal a quote from Lucius Annaeus Seneca.

called crime fortunate virtue

Successful and _____ _____ is

_____ _____.

Vice vs. Incompetence

Below is a group of words that, when properly arranged in the blanks, reveal a quote attributed to various sources, including Talleyrand.

blunder crime than worse

It is _____ _____ a

_____, it is a _____.

The Master Forger

The art world is agog! Six recently-sold paintings, each supposed to be by the hand of a different world-famous artist, have now been conclusively shown to be forgeries. Authorities believe the same "master forger" is behind all of this but they're still not sure who he or she actually is. Using only the clues available below, match each forged painting to the artist it was claimed to have been painted by, the country it was sold in, and the price it fetched at auction.

1. The Hal Garrison piece sold for four times as much money as "Cold Hills."

2. "Forever Blue" sold for twice as much as the painting sold in Portugal.

3. Of the piece that sold for $8,000,000 and the Inga Howell painting, one was "Cold Hills" and the other was sold in France.

4. The Inga Howell forgery wasn't sold in Spain.

5. "Baby Jane" (which wasn't passed off as a Margot Lane painting) fetched less money at auction than the piece that was sold in Portugal.

6. Of the painting sold in Germany and "Eighteen," one sold for 32 million dollars and the other was alleged to have been an early work by Greta Frank.

7. The Lyle Kramer painting fetched more money at auction than "Forever Blue," which was said to have been a Hal Garrison piece.

8. "Day of Night," the piece that sold for $2,000,000, and the painting that was sold in Norway were three different forgeries.

9. "Awestruck" didn't sell for either $2 million or $4 million.

10. The Freda Estes painting sold for $16,000,000, but not in Norway.

	Paintings						Countries						Artists					
	Awestruck	Baby Jane	Cold Hills	Day of Night	Eighteen	Forever Blue	Canada	France	Germany	Norway	Portugal	Spain	Freda Estes	Greta Frank	Hal Garrison	Inga Howell	Lyle Kramer	Margot Lane
Prices $1,000,000																		
$2,000,000																		
$4,000,000																		
$8,000,000																		
$16,000,000																		
$32,000,000																		
Artists Freda Estes																		
Greta Frank																		
Hal Garrison																		
Inga Howell																		
Lyle Kramer																		
Margot Lane																		
Countries Canada																		
France																		
Germany																		
Norway																		
Portugal																		
Spain																		

Prices	Paintings	Countries	Artists
$1,000,000			
$2,000,000			
$4,000,000			
$8,000,000			
$16,000,000			
$32,000,000			

COLD CASES

Three Quotes on Crime

These cryptograms are encoded using a type of substitution cipher called a Caesar shift. Each letter of the alphabet is replaced by another letter that is a fixed number of positions down the alphabet. For example, THE SMART CAT might become WKH VPDUW FDW with a Caesar shift of 3, where T becomes W, C becomes F, and so forth. With a Caesar shift of 4, it would become XLI WQEVX GEX. Each of the three quotes is shifted a different amount.

Noyzuxe . . . oy otjkkj rozzrk suxk zngt
znk xkmoyzkx ul znk ixosky, lurroky, gtj
soyluxzatky ul sgtqotj.
—Kjcgxj Mohhut

Wqepp lefmxw aipp tyvwyih fixmqiw / Qec
viegl xli hmkrmxc sj gvmqiw.
—Lerrel Qsvi

Xqqdwxudo ylfhv duh idwkhuhg eb rxu
khurlvp. Yluwxhv duh irufhg xsrq xv eb rxu
lpsxghqw fulphv.
—W.V. Holrw, "Jhurqwlrq"

Answers on page 187.

What Changed? (Part I)

Study this picture for 1 minute, then turn the page.

COLD CASES

What Changed? (Part II)

(Do not read this until you have read the previous page!)

From memory, can you tell what changed between this page and the previous page?

Answers on page 187.

The Suspect's Escape Route

You are standing at a crime scene in a building with only one exit. Elevators are local or express only; there are no stairs. What path did the suspect take to leave the building?

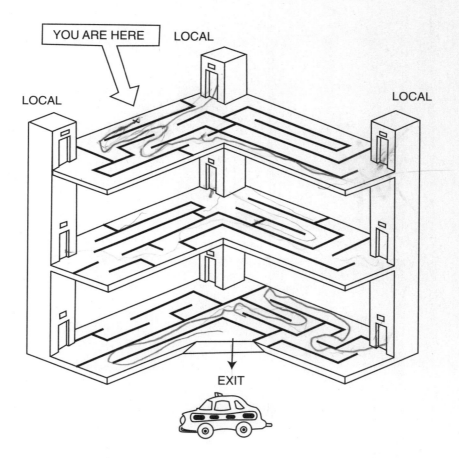

DNA Sequence

Examine the two images below carefully. Are these sequences a match or not?

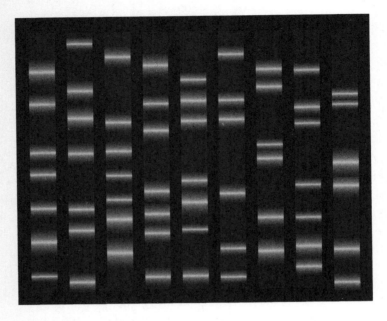

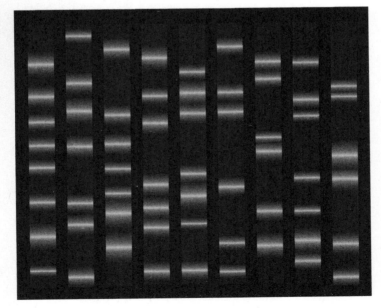

Answers on page 188.

The Redhead Murders (Part I)

Read this true crime account, and then turn to the next page to test your knowledge.

It sounds a bit like a Sherlock Holmes case, but it was deadly real. Between 1978 and 1992, particularly in 1984 and 1985, a serial killer murdered at least six women, and perhaps as many as eleven, with reddish or strawberry-blonde hair. The women's bodies were found on highways in a number of states including Tennessee, West Virginia, Pennsylvania, Kentucky, Arkansas, and Mississippi. Several of the women, who may have been hitchhikers or estranged from their families, have never been identified. One of the women was only identified in 2018; she was identified by a DNA match. While two male truck drivers were considered suspects at different time, both were eventually ruled out.

The Redhead Murders (Part II)

(Do not read this until you have read the previous page!)

1. The murderer operated primarily in this decade.

    A. 1970s

    B. 1980s

    C. 1990s

    D. 2000s

2. The killer operated in these states (check all that apply).

    _____ Tennessee

    _____ Kentucky

    _____ Kansas

    _____ New Jersey

3. What was the profession of both men who were considered suspects?

    A. Teachers

    B. Truck stop managers

    C. Truckers

    D. They were unemployed drifters.

Answers on page 188.

Tracing the Suspect

The suspect visited eight cities around the world. Can you put the list of the eight cities he visited in order, using the information below?

1. He went immediately from a city in Morocco to the capital city of an island country off Africa's southeastern coast.

2. Krakow was one of the first three cities.

3. Quito was one of the last three cities.

4. Kuala Lumpur was visited sometime after Prague and immediately before Singapore.

5. After visiting Antananarivo, he visited exactly two other cities before going to Barcelona.

6. Rabat was visited sometime after the city in the Czech Republic.

7. Singapore was visited sometime before the city in Ecuador, but not immediately before.

8. Poland was visited sometime before Prague.

9. Singapore was visited sometime before Spain.

Measuring Up

Accuracy is important when solving cases. Let's see how well you know your weights and measures. Pick out the correct equivalents from the lists:

1. One rod equals:
   a) 3 yards
   b) 1 serling
   c) $5\frac{1}{2}$ yards
   d) 10 feet

2. One league equals:
   a) 6 water miles
   b) 3 land miles
   c) 20,000 water inches
   d) 6 land miles

3. 16 drams equal:
   a) 1 drama
   b) 1 ounce
   c) 1 inch
   d) 1 centimeter

4. One peck equals:
   a) 8 picks
   b) 8 quarts
   c) 8 hugs
   d) 8 pounds

5. 20 grains equal:
   a) 1 scruple
   b) 1 spiffle
   c) 1 snuffle
   d) 1 farfel

6. One bolt equals:
   a) 40 shocks
   b) 40 yards
   c) 40 feet
   d) 40 miles

7. One carat equals:
   a) 200 millimeters
   b) 2 rings
   c) 200 milligrams
   d) one ounce

8. One cubit equals:
   a) $\frac{1}{10}$ arc
   b) 18 inches
   c) 36 inches
   d) 24 inches

9. One hand equals:
   a) $\frac{1}{2}$ foot
   b) 5 fingers
   c) 8 inches
   d) 4 inches

10. One pica equals:
    a) $\frac{1}{6}$ inch
    b) 16 inches
    c) 1.6 inches
    d) 160 inches

11. One ream equals:
    a) 144 sheets
    b) 256 sheets
    c) 500 sheets
    d) 100 sheets

12. One span equals:
    a) 1 bridge
    b) 180 feet
    c) 9 inches
    d) 9 yards

Answers on page 188.

COLD CASES

Find the Witness

There are 5 houses on Lakeside Drive. You need to follow up with two witnesses, Marie and Carolyn West, but the paperwork only lists their street, not the specific address. You know from the previous interview that the couple does not have children. The staff at the corner coffee shop and your own observations give you some clues. From the information given, can you find the right house?

A. Four of the houses are home to couples, and the other owned by a widow.

B. The retired couple and the Wests come in together frequently, but are not next-door neighbors.

C. The newlyweds are next-door neighbors to the Wests.

D. The widow is glad she doesn't have to mow the lawn for a corner lot.

E. The couple who just sent their kid off to college wish he were still home, so he could mow their corner lot. The newlyweds joke that they'll have their own little lawn-mower to take care of their corner lot in a few years.

| House A | House B | House C | House D | House E |

Answers on page 188.

COLD CASES

Where'd the Money Go?

This cryptogram is encoded using a type of substitution cipher called a Caesar shift. Each letter of the alphabet is replaced by another letter that is a fixed number of positions down the alphabet. For example, THE SMART CAT might become WKH VPDUW FDW with a Caesar shift of 3, where T becomes W, C becomes F, and so forth. With a Caesar shift of 4, it would become XLI WQEVX GEX.

Wv bpm mdmvqvo wn Vwdmujmz 24, 1971, i uiv kittqvo pquamtn Liv Kwwxmz (tibmz svwev ia L. J. Kwwxmz) pqriksml iv iqzxtivm, ivl lmuivlml $200,000 ivl nwcz xizikpcbma, epqkp pm zmkmqdml epmv bpm xtivm tivlml qv Amibbtm. Kwwxmz ittweml bpm xtivm'a xiaamvomza bw lqamujizs jcb bpmv wzlmzml bpm xqtwb bw ntg bw Umfqkw. Wvkm bpm xtivm pil oiqvml mvwcop itbqbclm, awumepmzm wdmz bpm Kiakilm Uwcvbiqva vmiz Ewwltivl, Eiapqvobwv, Kwwxmz rcuxml nzwu bpm xtivm ivl nmtt qvbw pqabwzg. Lmaxqbm i uiaaqdm uivpcvb, vw bzikm wn pqu pia mdmz jmmv nwcvl. Qv 1980, iv mqopb-gmiz-wtl jwg nwcvl vmiztg $6,000 qv zwbbqvo $20 jqtta tgqvo itwvo bpm jivsa wn bpm Kwtcujqi Zqdmz. I kpmks wn bpmqz amzqit vcujmza nwcvl bpib bpmg emzm xizb wn bpm zivawu uwvmg oqdmv bw Kwwxmz, jcb epib jmkium wn bpm zmab wn bpm uwvmg, ivl Kwwxmz, qa i ugabmzg bw bpqa lig.

Answers on page 189.

What Changed? (Part I)

Study this picture for 1 minute, then turn the page.

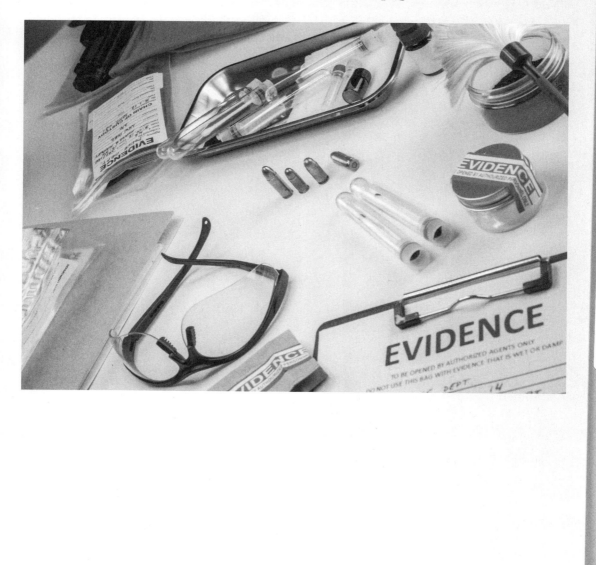

What Changed? (Part II)

(Do not read this until you have read the previous page!)

From memory, can you tell what changed between this page and the previous page?

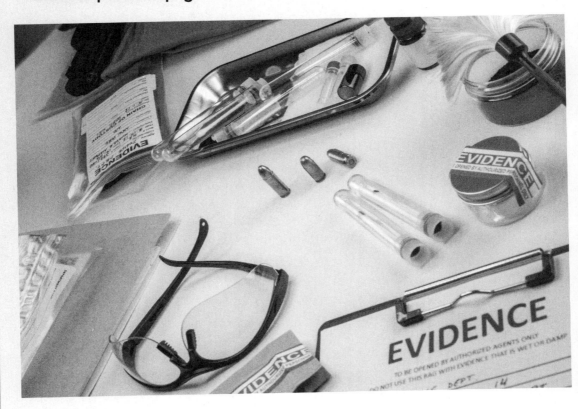

Answers on page 189.

COLD CASES

The Golden State Killer (Part I)

Read this account, and then turn to the next page to test your knowledge.

California's Sacramento County area was wracked with a series of violent rapes in the 1970s. The rapist planned each incident meticulously, even breaking into houses ahead of time to prepare for his entry later. The crimes ended in 1979 with no suspects.

Later that year, the area around Santa Barbara County experienced a terrifying series of murders. The killer often targeted couples, tying up the man, raping the woman, and murdering both. The killer stopped in 1986 without being caught.

It was not until 2001 that officials connected the rapist to the murderer. Entered into the criminal database, DNA from both crime sprees matched each other. Two big investigations become one massive one. This "Golden State Killer" had committed more than 50 rapes and at least 12 murders. But the DNA didn't match any person in the database, so there was still no suspect.

Then investigators turned from criminal DNA databases to genealogical ones. Investigators looked for familial matches to the killer's DNA in the open-source database GEDmatch. In 2018, they narrowed their results down to a solid suspect: Sacramento resident and one-time cop Joseph James DeAngelo. Officials compared the Golden State Killer's DNA to items taken from DeAngelo's trash and there it was, a perfect match. The Golden State Killer was caught.

COLD CASES

The Golden State Killer (Part II)

(Do not read this until you have read the previous page!)

1. How did investigators connect the Golden State Killer to Joseph James DeAngelo?

    A. Finding genealogical matches in an open-source database

    B. Matching the killer's DNA to DeAngelo's in the criminal database

    C. Catching him in the act of committing a crime

    D. A neighbor turned him in

2. When was the Golden State Killer active?

    A. In the early 2000s

    B. In the late 1990s

    C. In the 1970s and 1980s

    D. In the 1950s and 1960s

3. How did police determine both crime sprees were committed by the same person?

    A. They compared the M.O. in each case and determined they were similar.

    B. The DNA from both crime sprees matched in the criminal database.

    C. Witness descriptions of the criminal matched.

    D. Joseph James DeAngelo was a suspect in both investigations.

COLD CASES

Answers on page 189.

DNA Sequence

Examine the two images below carefully. Are these sequences a match or not?

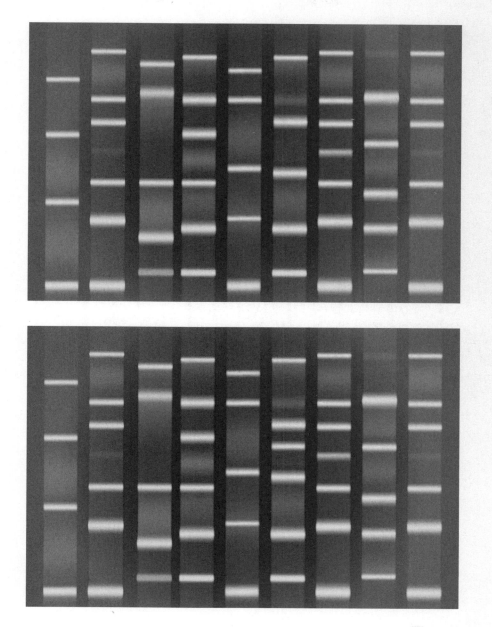

COLD CASES

Jean Racine on Crime

Below is a group of words that, when properly arranged in the blanks, reveal a quote from Jean Racine.

blossom degrees extreme like timid virtue was

Crime _____ _____ has its _____;

and _____ innocence _____ never known to

_____ suddenly into _____ license.

Resolving Crime

Below is a group of words that, when properly arranged in the blanks, reveal a quote from Thomas Henry Huxley.

mankind medicine other suffering wisdom

The only _____ for _____ ,
crime, and all the _____ woes of
_____ , is _____ .

Answers on page 189.

COLD CASES

Seen at the Scene (Part I)

Study this picture of the crime scene for 1 minute, then turn the page.

COLD CASES

Seen at the Scene (Part II)

(Do not read this until you have read the previous page!)

Which image exactly matches the picture from the previous page?

1

2

3

4

Answers on page 189.

Orner and Freiburger (Part I)

Read this account, and then turn to the next page to test your knowledge.

Late on February 28, 1961, cab driver John Orner drove to Fort Jackson in Columbia, South Carolina, to pick up a passenger. He never returned. His blood-covered cab turned up the next morning in downtown Columbia. Two days later, investigators found his body by the side of a road outside of town. He'd been shot in the head with a Harrington & Richardson (H&R) revolver.

One month later, an officer in Tennessee stopped 18-year-old Edward Freiburger for hitchhiking. Freiburger, a soldier at Fort Jackson, had gone AWOL on February 28. After finding an H&R revolver on him, the officer arrested him.

South Carolina investigators were intrigued. They found that Freiburger bought the gun the day the murder and then gone AWOL. He was based at Fort Jackson, Orner's last destination. But ballistics tests on the gun were inconclusive, so Freiburger was released. The case went cold.

Ballistics testing, however, improved. In 2000, an expert confirmed that Freiburger's gun had been used to kill John Orner. Freiburger was convicted of murder.

Case closed? Not quite. During the trial, Freiburger's lawyer never mentioned a 1961 investigator's note saying Freiburger's gun had not fired the bullet. This information could have changed the jury's decision. Freiburger was retried in 2015. The guilty verdict was overturned.

COLD CASES

Orner and Freiburger (Part II)

(Do not read this until you have read the previous page!)

1. John Orner's cab was found:

    A. Outside of Columbia

    B. In Tennessee

    C. In downtown Columbia

    D. Fort Jackson

2. What forensics technology was used in the 2000s to implicate Freibuger in the murder?

    A. Ballistics testing

    B. Blood spatter analysis

    C. Fingerprint analysis

    D. DNA testing

3. At the time of Freiburger's arrest in 1961, he:

    A. Was 18 years old

    B. Was a soldier

    C. Had a revolver

    D. All of the above

Answers on page 189.

COLD CASES

What Changed? (Part I)

Study this picture for 1 minute, then turn the page.

COLD CASES

What Changed? (Part II)

(Do not read this until you have read the previous page!)

From memory, can you tell what changed between this page and the previous page?

Answers on page 189.

DNA Sequence

Examine the two images below carefully. Are these sequences a match or not?

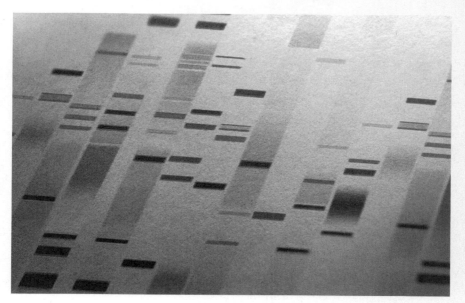

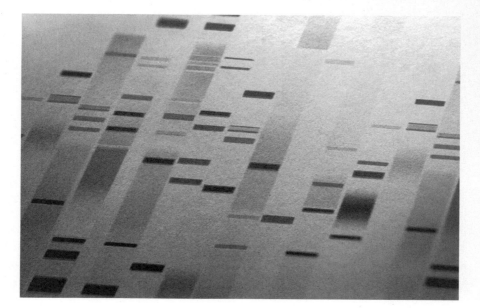

Answers on page 189.

Unlock the Safe

Crack the code to unlock the safe. The goal of this puzzle is to replace the question marks with a correct sequence of numbers. The numbers you need for the answer are contained in the rows above the question marks. Follow these 2 guides: A black dot indicates that a number needed for the solution is in that row and in the correct position; a white dot means that a number needed for the solution is in that row but in the wrong position. Numbers do not appear more than once in the solution, and the solution never begins with 0.

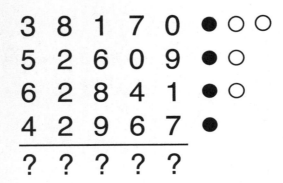

Answers on page 189.

Three Quotes on Crime

Cryptograms are messages in substitution code. Break the code to read the message. For example, THE SMART CAT might become FVO QWGDF JGF if **F** is substituted for **T, V** for **H, O** for **E,** and so on.

Poz kmzgpznp hc ztrdn gfj poz vhmnp
hc umrez rn ihtzmpx.
—Kzhmkz Qzmfgmj Nogv

Vordz pozmz rn g dhvzm udgnn R
ge rf rp, vordz pozmz rn g umrerfgd
zdzezfp R ge hc rp; vordz pozmz rn g
nhsd rf imrnhf, R ge fhp cmzz.
—Zskzfz Truphm Jzqn

Ozmz rn poz uogmerfk ztzfrfk, poz
umrerfgd'n cmrzfj.
—Uogmdzn Qgsjzdgrmz

Marked Bills

The local police have been tracking a series of marked bills that were stolen during a recent string of bank robberies, in an effort to capture the perpetrators. So far, five such bills have been located. Each was used in a different place and on a different day, and each bill was of a different denomination (such as a $10 or a $20). Using only the clues below, match each marked bill to the date and location in which it was spent, and determine the serial number and denomination of each one.

1. C-918303 was used 8 days after the bill that popped up in Midvale.
2. The $100 bill wasn't spent on April 13th.
3. P-101445 was either the $20 bill or the one used on April 5.
4. The $5 bill with the serial number B-492841 was used 4 days after F-667280, but not in Finsberg.
5. The Midvale bill was used 4 days after G-718428 was passed somewhere in Torbin.
6. The marked $20 bill was spent 4 days after the one in Nettleton.
7. Neither the $10 bill nor the $100 bill was used on April 1st.

		Serials					Locations					Denominations				
		B-492841	C-918303	F-667280	G-718428	P-101445	Finsberg	Midvale	Nettleton	Torbin	Uteville	$5	$10	$20	$50	$100
Dates	April 1															
	April 5															
	April 9															
	April 13															
	April 17															
Denominations	$5											
	$10											
	$20											
	$50											
	$100											
Locations	Finsberg						
	Midvale						
	Nettleton						
	Torbin						
	Uteville						

Dates	Serials	Locations	Denominations
April 1			
April 5			
April 9			
April 13			
April 17			

COLD CASES

DNA Sequence

Examine the two images below carefully. Are these sequences a match or not?

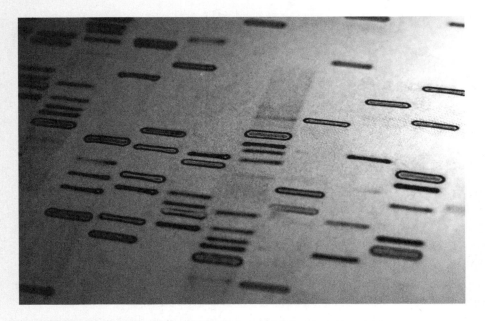

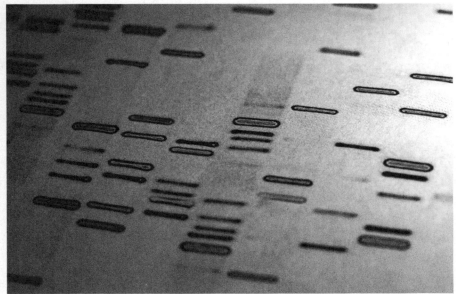

Answers on page 190.

Double Murder (Part I)

Read this account, and then turn to the next page to test your knowledge.

Lynda Mann and Dawn Ashworth were murdered in Leicestershire, England, in 1983 and 1986. Police suspected the same person committed both crimes. The girls were both 15 when they died. Both were raped and strangled. And in both investigations, police found semen of the same type.

Police arrested 17-year-old Richard Buckland in 1986. He had facts about Dawn's crime scene that were not public knowledge, and he kept confessing to Dawn's murder. He kept retracting this confession, however, and consistently denied murdering Lynda.

To strengthen the case against Richard, investigators turned to a brand-new technology: genetic fingerprinting. Experts found that the crime scene samples matched each other, but neither matched Richard. He was innocent.

Police still had to find their murderer. In 1987, Officials collected DNA samples from more than 5,000 local men. Not one matched. Then local Ian Kelly was overheard bragging that he had submitted his own DNA sample in place of a friend's. Police questioned Kelly, who quickly named the friend: Colin Pitchfork.

Police brought in Pitchfork, and he almost immediately confessed to both murders. To double check, experts compared his DNA to the crime scene samples—and everything matched. Pitchfork pleaded guilty the following January, ending the first murder investigation ever to use genetic fingerprinting.

COLD CASES

Double Murder (Part II)

(Do not read this until you have read the previous page!)

1. Who killed Lynda Mann and Dawn Ashworth?

    A. The case is unsolved

    B. Richard Buckland

    C. Colin Pitchfork

    D. Ian Kelly

2. None of the more than 5,000 DNA samples collected match the crime scene DNA because:

    A. Genetic fingerprinting was still new and faulty.

    B. The killer had not submitted his own DNA.

    C. Someone had contaminated the samples, making comparison impossible.

    D. Two different people had committed the murders.

3. When police questioned the murderer in 1987:

    A. He confessed to both murders.

    B. He confessed to Dawn's murder, but not Lynda's .

    C. He confessed to Lynda's murder, but not Dawn's.

    D. He denied any involvement in the murders.

Answers on page 190.

What Changed? (Part I)

Study this picture for 1 minute, then turn the page.

COLD CASES

What Changed? (Part II)

(Do not read this until you have read the previous page!)

From memory, can you tell what changed between this page and the previous page?

Answers on page 190.

A Notorious Murder

Cryptograms are messages in substitution code. Break the code to read the message. For example, THE SMART CAT might become FVO QWGDF JGF if **F** is substituted for **T, V** for **H, O** for **E,** and so on.

Ci rah hnpfw akspq km Gnpza 9, 1997, cimfshircnf pnl nprcqr Zapcqrklahp Unffnzh, nfqk eikui nq Xcjjch Qgnffq kp Ikrkpcksq X.C.J., unq jsiihb bkui xw n bpcth-xw qakkrhp ksrqcbh rah Lhrhpqhi Nsrkgkrcth Gsqhsg ki Ucfqacph Xksfhtnpb. Unffnzh unq nr rah gsqhsg rk nrrhib rah nmrhp-lnprw mkp "Tcxh" gnjnycih'q Qksf Rpnci Gsqcz Nunpbq. Nr npksib 12:30 N.G., Unffnzh fhmr rah hthir ucra acq hirkspnjh. Uahi acq thaczfh qrkllhb nr n phb fcjar dsqr 50 wnpbq mpkg rah gsqhsg, n xfnze Zahtw Cglnfn lsffhb nfkijqcbh, nib rah bpcthp mcphb isghpksq pksibq mpkg n 9gg lcqrkf, acrrcij rah 24-whnp-kfb pnl qrnp ci rah zahqr. Acq gspbhp phgnciq siqkfthb, nfraksja lfhirw km zkiqlcpnzw rahkpchq qsppksib acq bhnra.

The Suspect's Escape Route

You are standing at a crime scene in a building with only one exit.
Elevators are local or express only; there are no stairs. What path did
the suspect take to leave the building?

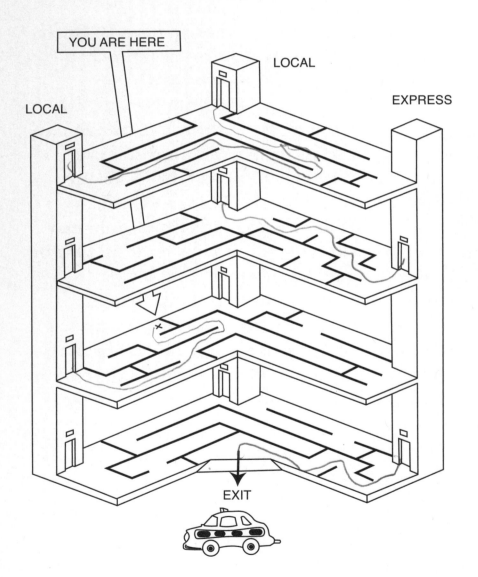

Answers on page 190.

Seen at the Scene (Part I)

Study this picture of the crime scene for 1 minute, then turn the page.

Seen at the Scene (Part II)

(Do not read this until you have read the previous page!)

Which image exactly matches the crime scene?

1

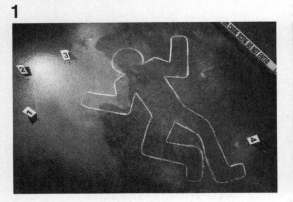

2

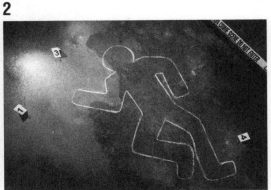

3

4

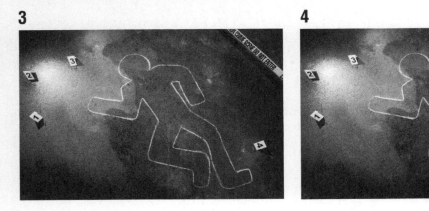

Answers on page 190.

COLD CASES

DNA Sequence

Examine the two images below carefully. Are these sequences a match or not?

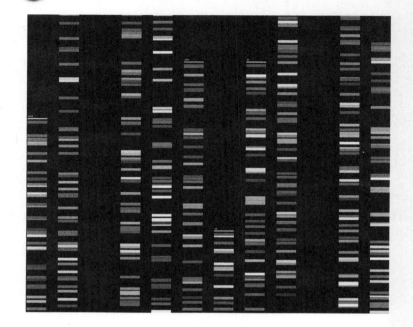

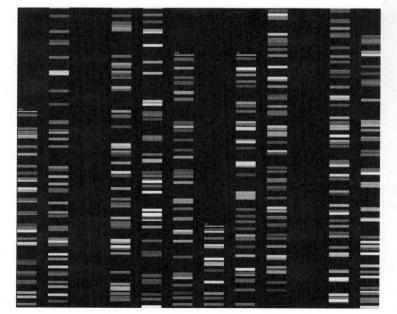

COLD CASES

Stolen Street Signs

Someone's been stealing street signs in Starrington! Every week (always on a Saturday night) a new sign has gone missing. Each time it's a different type of sign (stop sign, yield sign, etc.) in a different part of town. Help the police track down the thief by matching each sign to the date it went missing and its original location at the intersection of two streets.

1. Of the speed limit sign and the one that was at Barnacle Road, one went missing on July 25th and the other was at the corner of Tarragon Lane.

2. Quinella Street doesn't intersect with Falstaff St.

3. The speed limit sign was stolen sometime after the one from Ralston Avenue.

4. The Amble Lane sign didn't go missing on August 1st.

5. The Dwight Street sign went missing one week before the one from Tarragon Lane.

6. The one-way sign was stolen 1 week before the Casper Boulevard sign, and 3 weeks before the one on Selby Street.

7. The dead end sign, the stop sign, the one from Selby Street, and the two stolen before July 14th were five different signs.

8. One of the missing signs stood at the corner of Selby Street and Barnacle Road. Selby Street doesn't have any "No Parking" signs.

9. Peabody Lane, which has no "Dead End" signs anywhere near it, intersects with either Dwight Street or Everett Avenue (but not both).

10. The stop sign went missing sometime before the sign at Peabody Lane (but not on July 18th).

	Signs						Streets						Streets					
	Dead End	No Parking	One Way	Speed Limit	Stop	Yield	Amble Ln.	Barnacle Rd.	Casper Blvd.	Dwight St.	Everett Ave.	Falstaff St.	Oracle Rd.	Peabody Ln.	Quinella St.	Ralston Ave.	Selby St.	Tarragon Ln.
Dates July 4th																		
July 11th																		
July 18th																		
July 25th																		
August 1st																		
August 8th																		
Streets Oracle Rd.																		
Peabody Ln.																		
Quinella St.																		
Ralston Ave.																		
Selby St.																		
Tarragon Ln.																		
Streets Amble Ln.																		
Barnacle Rd.																		
Casper Blvd.																		
Dwight St.																		
Everett Ave.																		
Falstaff St.																		

Dates	Signs	Streets	Streets
July 4th			
July 11th			
July 18th			
July 25th			
August 1st			
August 8th			

Find the Witness

On Chicago Avenue, there are 5 houses that are identical to each other. You need to follow up with a witness, Jimmy Perez, but without any address on the doors you are not sure which house to approach. You know that from a previous statement that Perez lives with his husband and has no children. The staff at the corner coffee shop and your own observations give you some clues. From the information given, can you find the right house?

A. **One staff member says that Perez drives a compact and his husband has an SUV.**

B. **They do not have a motorcycle but are interested in buying one, and have said they'll get advice from their next door neighbor.**

C. **Houses A and E have motorcycles in front of them.**

D. **House B has a minivan parked in front of it and children's toys in the yard.**

House A   House B   House C   House D   House E

Answers on page 191.

Justice at Last (Part I)

Read this account, and then turn to the next page to test your knowledge.

In June of 1968, James Keuler was found stabbed to death in his Seattle apartment. Investigators collected blood, which provided a DNA profile, as well as a broken knife blade and footprints. But nothing led detectives to the killer.

About four years later and not far away, Jackson and Daisy Schley returned home to find a man in their apartment. The man shot Jackson, then abducted and raped Daisy. Investigators collected the perpetrator's DNA from Daisy's clothing, but the case was left unsolved.

These cases seemed completely different. You can imagine the surprise when, in 2005, Washington's crime lab discovered the DNA from the crimes matched. But this DNA profile didn't match any criminal in the database. The cases went cold again.

There was finally a hit in 2009. At 72 years old, Samuel Evans was finishing up a sentence for sexual assault in Nevada and moving back home to the Seattle area. As a sex offender, he had to submit a DNA sample for the criminal database. When added, Evans's sample matched the DNA profile in the Keuler and Schley cases. Evans was convicted two years later with a 20-year prison sentence. Investigators finally had their man.

Justice at Last (Part II)

(Do not read this until you have read the previous page!)

1. In 2005, Washington's crime lab discovered:

   A. The DNA found at Keuler's apartment matched Samuel Evans.

   B. Fingerprints found on the scene in both cases matched each other.

   C. DNA connected to the Keuler and Schley cases matched.

   D. Evidence found in the Schley case was unusable.

2. What was found in Keuler's apartment that ultimately led investigators to his killer?

   A. Blood

   B. Fingerprints

   C. Footprints

   D. An eyewitness

3. Why was Evans's DNA added to the database in 2009?

   A. He was a suspect in another murder.

   B. He was a registered sex offender.

   C. He was arrested for a traffic violation.

   D. Investigators suspected he had murdered James Keuler.

Answers on page 191.

COLD CASES

Overheard Information (Part I)

Read the story below, then turn the page and answer the questions.

A woman at a doctor's office overheard another woman talking on her cell phone about what sounded like a crime that had been committed long ago. The woman said, "The thing is, Danny wasn't at our house that night. We said he was because Danny's friend Tim was my husband's boss and threatened to fire us if we caused problems for Danny. And Tim swore that Danny had been with John that night, but hanging out with John would violate his parole terms, so he claimed to be at our house instead. Tim swore he didn't steal anything that night. And maybe he didn't! But my husband doesn't work for Tim anymore, and so I wonder if I should go to the cops or if that just opens a can of worms."

Overheard Information (Part II)

(Do not read this until you have read the previous page!

1. Where was the woman who was talking on the phone?

    A. Library

    B. Train

    C. Bus

    D. Doctor's office

2. Who did Tim tell the speaker Danny was hanging out with on the night of the crime?

    A. Jim

    B. Tim

    C. John

    D. Danny was alone

3. What crime was committed that night?

    A. Murder

    B. Theft

    C. Carjacking

    D. Assault

COLD CASES

Answers on page 191.

DNA Sequence

Examine the two images below carefully. Are these sequences a match or not?

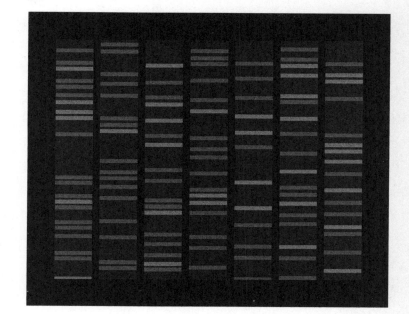

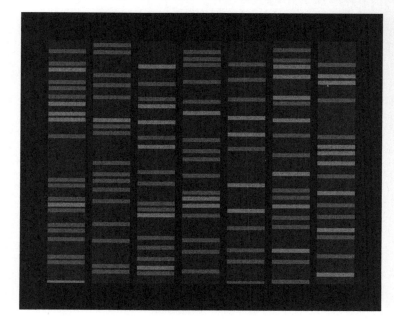

Finally Solved

Cryptograms are messages in substitution code. Break the code to read the message. For example, THE SMART CAT might become FVO QWGDF JGF if **F** is substituted for **T, V** for **H, O** for **E,** and so on.

Bi Cqiv 1990, r zmbsvm fjm pav Rmhjmvz Hjpjm Ovmsbgv jf Rhvmbgr (RHOR) riz abo fvhrev krmpivm opjkkvz fjm tmvrdfrop rp r gjisvibvigv opjmv ivrm Mjgavopvm, Ivu Xjmd. Uabev pav fvhrev nqrmz uvip bipj pav opjmv, r triz jf rmhvz pabvsvo rpprgdvz pav zmbsvm, urbpvz fjm pav fvhrev nqrmz pj mvpqmi, pavi jmzvmvz pavh pj zmbsv pav pmqgd pj ri qiirhvz ejgrpbji, uavmv pav pabvsvo pmriofvmmvz pav hjivx pj r urbpbin sri, pbvz qk pav puj nqrmzo, riz vogrkvz ubpa pav hjivx. Pav pjpre arqe jf $10.8 hbeebji mridvz ro jiv pav ermnvop avbopo bi abopjmx. Pav mjttvmx uro reoj ijpvujmpax fjm pav frgp parp bp mvhrbivz qiojesvz fjm hjmv pari r zvgrzv. Bi 2002, pajqna, pav zmbsvm jf pav mjttvz RHOR pmqgd, Retvmp Mribvmb, rzhbppvz pj hropvmhbizbin pav ogavhv.

Answers on page 191.

What Changed? (Part I)

Study this picture for 1 minute, then turn the page.

COLD CASES

What Changed? (Part II)

(Do not read this until you have read the previous page!)

From memory, can you tell what changed between this page and the previous page?

Answers on page 191.

The Suspect's Escape Route

You are standing at a crime scene in a building with only one exit. Elevators are local or express only; there are no stairs. What path did the suspect take to leave the building?

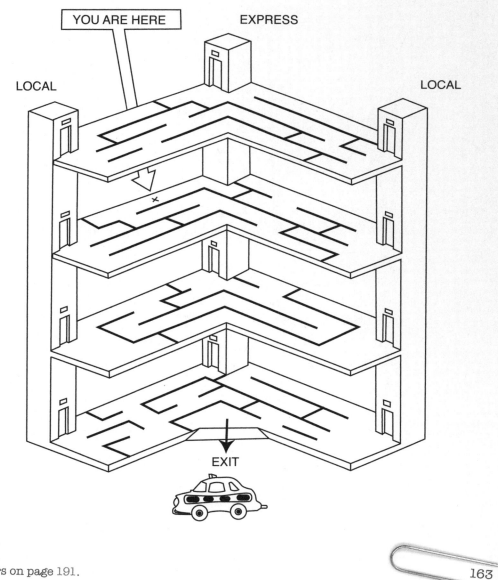

What Is History?

Below is a group of words that, when properly arranged in the blanks, reveal a quote from Voltaire.

history more no of misfortunes portrayal

_____ is _____ _____
than the _____ _____ crimes
and _____ .

Crime in Poetry

Below is a group of words that, when properly arranged in the blanks, reveal a quote from the poet Lord Byron in "The Corsair."

crimes left linked name other thousand virtue

He _____ a corsair's _____ to
_____ times,

_____ with one _____, and a
_____ _____.

Answers on page 192.

The Expanding Case of Samuel Little (Part I)

Read this account, and then turn to the next page to test your knowledge.

Born in 1940, Samuel Little spent most of his life as a nomad, shoplifting to support himself as he moved around. He had run-ins with the police—for stealing, drugs, solicitation, and even a couple of accusations of murder—but spent little time in jail.

Then in 2012, police arrested him at a homeless shelter in Kentucky. He was wanted for a narcotics charge in California. When he arrived in Los Angeles, the LAPD took a DNA sample for their records. It had three unexpected matches to cold cases from the 1980s. All of them were homicide. Little swore he was innocent, but by 2014, he was serving three life sentences for murdering three women in California.

Fast forward four years. The FBI had reviewed Little's murders and noticed similarities to other cold cases, especially one in Texas. Texas Rangers interviewed Little in May 2018 and got a waterfall of revelations. Little confessed in detail to more than 90 murders in 14 states. He even drew pictures of his victims. Over the next year, investigators across the country confirmed 34 of the murders, then 60. The number kept growing. The more they learned, the more Little looked like the most prolific serial killer in U.S. history.

The Expanding Case of Samuel Little (Part II)

(Do not read this until you have read the previous page!)

1. What was Little arrested for in 2012?
    A. Murder
    B. Solicitation
    C. Shoplifting
    D. Narcotics

2. How many murders were part of Little's original conviction in 2014?
    A. Four
    B. Three
    C. Sixty
    D. Thirty-four

3. To what agency did Little first confess in 2018?
    A. Texas Rangers
    B. LAPD
    C. FBI
    D. Kentucky police

Answers on page 192.

Seen at the Scene (Part I)

Study this picture of the crime scene for 1 minute, then turn the page.

COLD CASES

Seen at the Scene (Part II)

(Do not read this until you have read the previous page!)

Which image exactly matches the picture from the previous page?

1   2

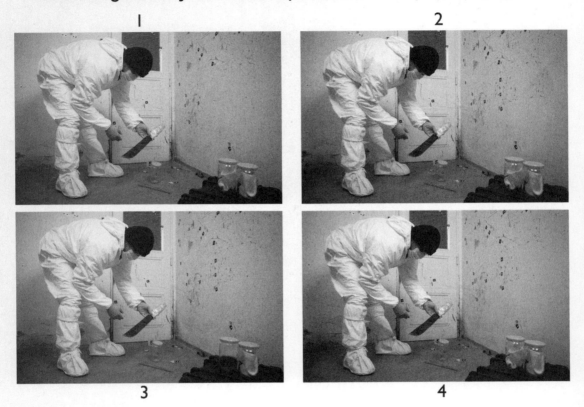

3   4

Answers on page 192.

COLD CASES

From Opened to Closed

letter on each line to go from the top word to the bottom word. Do not change the order of the letters. You must have a common English word at each step.

OPENED

_____

_____

Delivers one's opinion

_____

_____

_____

Looks at intently

_____

_____

_____

_____

A bride or a light might have done this

_____

_____

_____

Common ingredient in mulled wine

_____

CLOSED

COLD CASES

DNA Sequence

Examine the two images below carefully. Are these sequences a match or not?

Answers on page 192.

What Changed? (Part I)

Study this picture for 1 minute, then turn the page.

What Changed? (Part II)

(Do not read this until you have read the previous page!)

From memory, can you tell what changed between this page and the previous page?

Answers on page 192.

Unlock the Safe

Crack the code and unlock the safe. The goal of this puzzle is to replace the question marks with a correct sequence of numbers. The numbers you need for the answer are contained in the rows above the question marks. Follow these 2 guides: A black dot indicates that a number needed for the solution is in that row and in the correct position; a white dot means that a number needed for the solution is in that row but in the wrong position. Numbers do not appear more than once in the solution, and the solution never begins with 0.

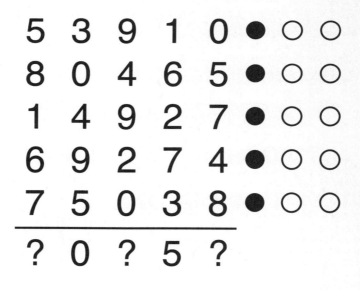

$$5 \quad 3 \quad 9 \quad 1 \quad 0 \quad \bullet \; \circ \; \circ$$
$$8 \quad 0 \quad 4 \quad 6 \quad 5 \quad \bullet \; \circ \; \circ$$
$$1 \quad 4 \quad 9 \quad 2 \quad 7 \quad \bullet \; \circ \; \circ$$
$$6 \quad 9 \quad 2 \quad 7 \quad 4 \quad \bullet \; \circ \; \circ$$
$$7 \quad 5 \quad 0 \quad 3 \quad 8 \quad \bullet \; \circ \; \circ$$
$$\overline{}$$
$$? \quad 0 \quad ? \quad 5 \quad ?$$

Find the Witness

On Plum Street, there are 5 houses. You need to follow up with a witness, Melanie Shah, but the paperwork only lists her street, not the specific address. You know that Shah is a divorced woman who lives by herself. The staff at the coffee shop around the corner and your own observations give you some clues. From the information given, can you find the right house?

A. One member of the wait staff says Shah recently mentioned repainting her house blue. There are two blue houses on the street.

B. Another member of the wait staff knows that a family lives in house D.

C. House B is yellow.

D. House C is green.

E. House E is white.

House A

House B

House C

House D

House E

Answers on page 192.

Seen at the Scene (Part I)

Study this picture of the crime scene for 1 minute, then turn the page.

COLD CASES

Seen at the Scene (Part II)

(Do not read this until you have read the previous page!)

Which image exactly matches the picture from the previous page?

1.

2.

3.

4.

Answers on page 192.

Fingerprint Match

Find the matching fingerprint(s). There may be more than one.

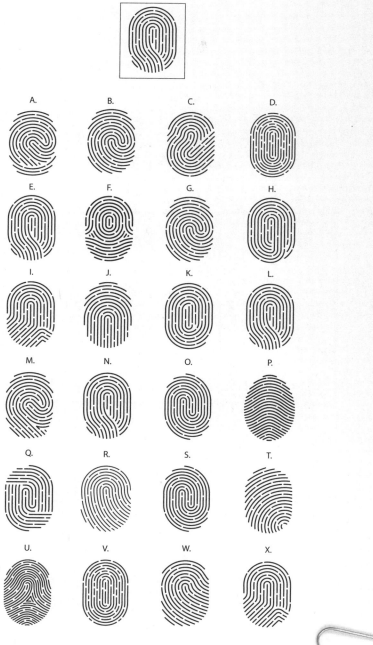

Motel Hideout

A thief hides out in one of the 45 motel rooms listed in the chart below. The motel's in-house detective received a sheet of four clues, signed "The Logical Thief." Using these clues, the detective found the room number within 15 minutes—but by that time, the thief had fled. Can you find the thief's motel room quicker?

1. **Both digits are odd.**
2. **The first digit is equal to or greater than the second digit.**
3. **The sum of the digits is 5 or less.**
4. **The first digit is not divisible by 3.**

51	52	53	54	55	56	57	58	59
41	42	43	44	45	46	47	48	49
31	32	33	34	35	36	37	38	39
21	22	23	24	25	26	27	28	29
11	12	13	14	15	16	17	18	19

Answers on page 192.

Answers

Find a Lead (page 4)
Answers may vary. FIND, fend, lend, LEAD

Cold Case (page 4)
Answers may vary. COLD, hold, hole, home, come, came, CASE

Cold Case Cryptogram (page 5)
Between 2005 and 2009, the bodies of eight young women were found in or near Jennings, Louisiana, several in canals. Because the bodies of the victims, called the Jennings 8, were badly decomposed, the cause of death could not always be determined. Many of the women knew each other. While several people have been arrested in connection with the case, all suspects were eventually released for lack of evidence. No trial has ever taken place.

The Suspect's Escape Route (page 6)

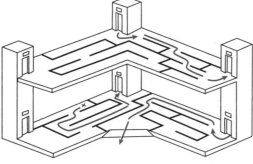

Fingerprint Match (page 7)
The matching pairs are: A and K; B and E; C and F; D and I; G and L; H and J.

Cold Case Anagrams (page 8)
crime scene; unsolved; suspect

Cold Case Anagrams (page 8)
evidence; detective; task force

Find the Witness (page 9)
Patel is in house B.

DNA Sequence (page 10)

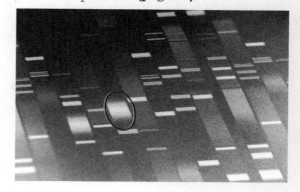

Seen at the Scene (pages 11-12)
Picture 4 is a match.

The First Instance (page 13)
Whatever the punishment, once a specific crime has appeared for the first time, its reappearance is more likely than its initial emergence could have been.

The Role of the State (page 13)
A state is not a mere society, having a common place, established for the prevention of mutual crime and for the sake of exchange.

Answers

Wrongs Righted (page 14)

Founded in 1992 by Barry Scheck and Peter Neufeld, the Innocence Project aims to examine old cases and gather new evidence, especially DNA evidence, that might exonerate people who have been wrongfully convicted of crimes. False eyewitness accounts have led to some wrongful convictions, along with the cases of people who pleaded guilty to a crime they had not committed in order to garner a lighter sentence. More than 350 people have been freed on DNA evidence because of the project's dogged pursuit of justice. The project began as part of a law school's project, but continues today as a non-profit organization. Thousands of prisoners ask the Innocence Project to take their case; a thorough review of the case takes place before the Innocence Project begins work.

The Case of Elizabeth Short
(pages 15–16)
1. D; 2. A; 3. D

What Changed? (pages 17–18)
A pair of tweezers disappeared. Look to the right of the scissors in the bottom half of the suitcase.

DNA Sequence (page 19)

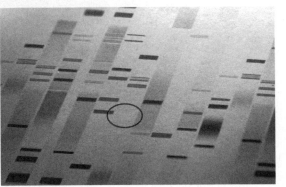

Without a Trace (page 20)

Was it crime? Was it aliens? Was it the paranormal? Between 1945 and 1950, five people disappeared in the area near Bennington, Vermont. A local author described it as the "Bennington Triangle." A 74-year-old hunter died while guide a group of fellow hunters up a mountain, perhaps accidentally drowned. An 18-year-old college student died when she was hiking. A veteran disappeared from a bus stop as he returned home to the Bennington area, his belongings left behind on the bus. A child disappeared in 1950 from a vehicle. Just a few weeks after the boy's disappearance, a 53-year-old woman disappeared while hiking. Her body, unlike that of the others, was eventually found.

The Case of Betty Gail Brown (pages 21–22)
1. A; 2. B; 3. 1965

The Suspect's Escape Route (page 23)

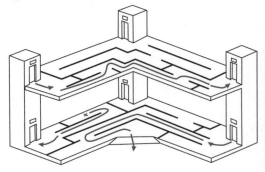

Answers

Find a Body (page 24)
Answers may vary. FIND, bind, bond, bony, BODY

Get a Lead in the Case
(page 24)
Answers may vary. LEAD, lend, lent, cent, cant, cast, CASE

What Changed? (pages 25–26)
The scissors in the top of case disappeared.

Crime Anagrams (page 27)
analysis; fiber; bloodstain

Crime Anagrams (page 27)
tipline; reward; witness

The Jewel Thief's Shopping List (pages 28–29)
The leftover letters spell: "Diamonds are a girl's best friend."

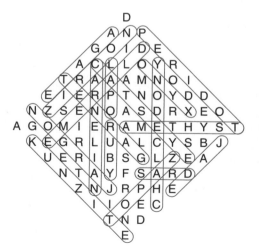

DNA Sequence (page 30)

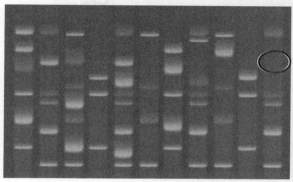

Killing in Depression-Era Cleveland (page 32)
1. False; 2. D; 3. B

What Changed? (pages 33–34)
A bullet casing disappeared. See the bottom center portion of the picture.

Genetic Fingerprints (pages 35–36)
1. B; 2. D; 3. A

DNA Sequence (page 37)

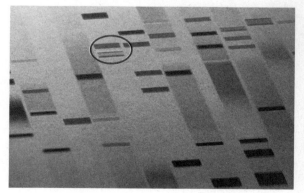

COLD CASES

Answers

A Famous Disappearance (page 38)

In 1975, labor leader Jimmy Hoffa disappeared on his way to a Detroit-area restaurant. Hoffa was the president of the Teamsters Union during the 1950s and 1960s. In 1964, he went to jail for bribing a grand juror investigating corruption in the union. In 1971, he was released on the condition that he not participate in any further union activity. Hoffa was preparing a legal challenge to that injunction when he disappeared on July 30, 1975. He was last seen in the parking lot of the Machus Red Fox Restaurant.

Hoffa had strong connections to the Mafia, and several mobsters have claimed that he met a grisly end on their say so. Although his body has never been found, authorities officially declared him dead on July 30, 1982. As recently as November 2006, the FBI dug up farmland in Michigan hoping to turn up a corpse. So far, no luck.

The Case of Carolyn Wasilewski (pages 39–40)

1. False; 2. False; 3. True

What Changed? (pages 41–42)

A packet of money disappeared (top center).

Seen at the Scene (pages 43–44)

Picture 2 is a match.

Find the Witness (page 45)

Ken Rawlins and his wife are found in house E.

Don't Miss a Clue (page 46)

Answers may vary. MISS, mist, most, cost, coat, goat, gout, glut, glue, CLUE

Mayhem on Wall Street (page 47–48)

1. D; 2. C; 3. A

DNA Sequence (page 49)

They are a match.

The Suspect's Escape Route (page 50)

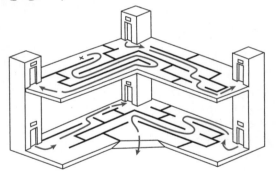

What Changed? (pages 51–52)

The handle to the tool disasppeared (bottom center portion of picture).

COLD CASES

Answers

Crime Anagrams (page 53)
homicide; battery; weapon

Virgil on Crime (page 53)
Had I a thousand tongues, a hundred mouths, a voice of iron and a chest of brass, I could not tell all the forms of crime, could not name all the types of punishment.

DNA Sequence (page 54)
They are a match.

The Connecticut River Valley Killer (pages 55-56)
1. C; 2. C; 3. D

What Changed? (pages 57-58)
The pad and pencil to the right of the typewriter disappeared.

Without a Trace (page 59)
The name Louis Aimé Augustin Le Prince doesn't mean much to most people, but some believe he was the first person to record moving images on film, a good seven years before Thomas Edison. Whether or not he did so is open to debate, as is what happened to him on September 16, 1890. On that day, Le Prince's brother accompanied him to the train station in Dijon, France, where he was scheduled to take the express train to Paris. When the train reached Paris, however, Le Prince and his luggage were nowhere to be found. The train was searched, as were the tracks between Dijon and Paris, but no sign of Le Prince or his luggage was ever found. Theories about his disappearance range from his being murdered for trying to fight Edison over the patent of the first motion picture to his family forcing him to go into hiding to keep him safe from people who wanted his patents for themselves. Others believe that Le Prince took his own life because he was nearly bankrupt.

A Motive for Murder (page 60)

DNA Sequence (page 62)

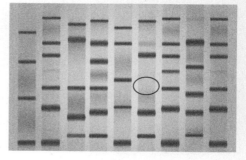

DNA Quiz (page 63)
1. A; 2. Adenine, guanine, thymine; 3. A

The Cat Burglar (pages 64-65)

Years	Cities	Items	Months
1963	London	sapphires	October
1970	Berlin	gold bars	September
1977	Vancouver	emeralds	July
1984	Paris	cash	June
1991	Antwerp	diamonds	April
1998	Seattle	rubies	May

COLD CASES

Answers

The Suspect's Escape Route
(page 66)

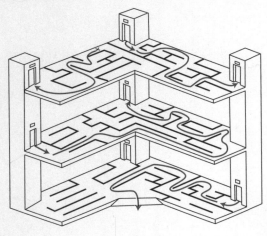

What Changed? (pages 67-68)
The ruler near the phone disappeared.

Will New Clues Lead to a Break in the Case? (page 69)
Answers may vary. CLUES, flues, flies, flied, fried, freed, breed, bread, BREAK

DNA Sequence (page 70)
They are a match.

The Great Plains Butcher
(pages 71-72)
1. B; 2. D; 3. B

Find the Witness (page 73)
White lives in house C.

Fingerprint Match (page 74)
The matching pairs are: A and K; B and I; C and L; D and J; E and H; F and N; G and P; M and O

What Changed? (pages 75-76)
The contents of the plastic bag in the front disappeared.

Seen at the Scene (pages 77-78)
Picture 1 is a match.

DNA Sequence (page 79)

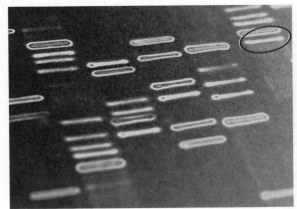

Unlock the Safe (page 80)
726

The Zodiac Killer (pages 81-82)
1. False; 2. A; 3. B

What Changed? (pages 83-84)
The police officer standing at the head of the chalk outline walked away.

Answers

Dizzier Noble (page 85)

Massachusetts; Fall River; Andrew (Lizzie's father); Abby Borden (Lizzie's stepmother); Bridget; hatchet; forty whacks; stepmother

The Suspect's Escape Route

(page 86)

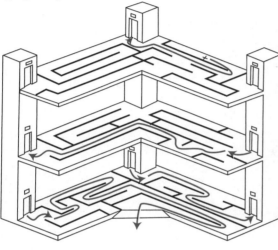

Tracing the Suspect (page 87)

The order is: Charleston, South Carolina; Topeka, Kansas; Oklahoma City, Oklahoma; Baltimore, Maryland; Milwaukee, Wisconsin; San Diego, California; Boise, Idaho; Atlanta, Georgia.

Parallel Words (page 88)

C. Thick

Sorry for Their Crimes? (page 88)

Sympathetic. It means to be compassionate, while the rest mean to be sorry for one's own sins.

DNA Sequence (page 89)

They are a match.

An Effective Deterrence?

(page 90)

The fear of ignominious death, I believe, never deterred anyone from the commission of a crime, because in committing it the mind is roused to activity about present circumstances.

From the Aeneid (page 90)

From a single crime know the nation.

What Changed? (pages 91-92)

Writing on the evidence tag beneath the clipboard has disappeared.

Seen at the Scene (pages 93-94)

Picture 4 is a match.

DNA Sequence (page 95)

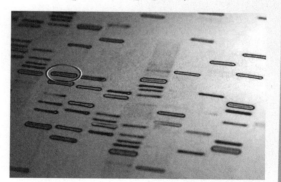

Answers

A Murder in Vegas (pages 96-97)

```
J K D Y E W L B K C U L D O O G A
S Q H A Z A R D K W D I V V B E U
J Y A P A S B A M N D M E T S T Y
B E Z A J A Z Y D A N O N S D N R
E L L S D K X U Z O S D T B E A X
T Y E L L Y E G I P K D U X P H D
P O U Z T D A T E P C S R P P N J
H C S J M M A C E B U H E E D X S
K D C S B L U N C E R T A I N T Y
G V J L U L Z W K T N G J N T V T
O O E C A P F I T P X E G I C N E
Y U L T T E M P T F O R T U N E B
O A I R S U X N W P T V E H F W C
C O Z T R Z U K A G J K O G A L T
N L D A N G E R Z B J S J G D A S
P J H C E A D S B C X I E K S C K
I O G I A Y B M Q G G R A M A E J
```

A Disappearance in 1910
(page 98)

After spending most of December 12, 1910, shopping in Manhattan, American socialite Dorothy Arnold told a friend she was planning to walk home through Central Park. She never made it. Fearing their daughter had eloped with her one-time boyfriend George Griscom, Jr., the Arnolds immediately hired the Pinkerton Detective Agency, although they did not report her missing to police until almost a month later. Once the press heard the news, theories spread like wildfire, most of them pointing the finger at Griscom. Some believed he had murdered Arnold, but others thought she had died as the result of a botched abortion. Still others felt her family had banished her to Switzerland and then used her disappearance as a cover-up. No evidence was ever found to formally charge Griscom, and Arnold's disappearance remains unsolved.

What Changed? (pages 99-100)
The poster in the bottom left corner of the picture has changed.

DNA Sequence (page 101)
They are a match.

The Suspect's Escape Route
(page 102)

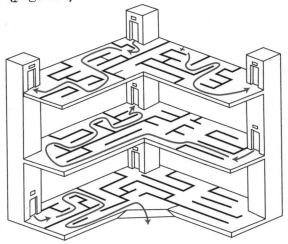

Seen at the Scene (pages 103-104)
Picture 2 is a match.

Jar Etch Kipper (page 105)
Whitechapel; Scotland Yard; prostitutes; ripperology; leather apron; East End; canonical five; Dear Boss; Saucy Jacky; From Hell; George Lusk

COLD CASES

The Poison Was Found in the... (pages 106-107)

```
V X R A X D U D D F O N D U E
C W W B O K W O U C I T E F S
X H O D M C O M P O T E A T F
I S A W R F O C M O U S S E O
C V B P L J R C D K M M K S T
I Z Q E A U B U S I M A R I T
N D G N L T L Q C E G E E E I
G N O L D C I C V X I R Q E T
A P E N I J N F E K A C P U C
T R R K T O I E P Y N D A F E
E O F A U T T E E T Z E K P J
A F O G D R B E R R Y S N W W
U I A O O R D I C C V P A H W
X T U T T I F R U T T I L R N
L E N O I L G A B A Z H A U C M
B R L T E Y R T S A P W D C O C
F O E J E I N W O R B F E F F H
L L O R S S I W S J D K K P H
P E A C H M E L B A K L A V A
N G I N G E R B R E A D B C F
```

DNA Sequence (page 108)
They are a match.

A Murder in Sweden
(pages 109-110)
1. B; 2. B; 3. C

A Quip from Seneca (page 111)
Successful and fortunate crime is called virtue.

Vice vs. Incompetence (page 111)
It is worse than a crime, it is a blunder.

The Master Forger (pages 112-113)

Prices	Paintings	Countries	Artists
$1,000,000	Baby Jane	Germany	Greta Frank
$2,000,000	Cold Hills	Canada	Inga Howell
$4,000,000	Day of Night	Portugal	Margot Lane
$8,000,000	Forever Blue	France	Hal Garrison
$16,000,000	Awestruck	Spain	Freda Estes
$32,000,000	Eighteen	Norway	Lyle Kramer

Three Quotes on Crime
(page 114)
History... is indeed little more than the register of the crimes, follies, and misfortunes of mankind.
—Edward Gibbon (Caesar shift of 6)

Small habits well pursued betimes / May reach the dignity of crimes.
—Hannah More (Caesar shift of 4)

Unnatural vices are fathered by our heroism. Virtues are forced upon us by our impudent crimes.
—T.S. Eliot, "Gerontion" (Caesar shift of 3)

What Changed? (pages 115-116)
An extra ruler appeared (behind marker 2).

COLD CASES

Answers

The Suspect's Escape Route
(page 117)

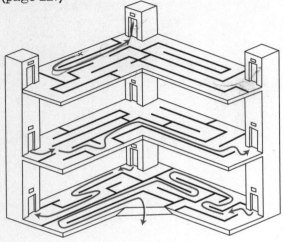

DNA Sequence (page 118)

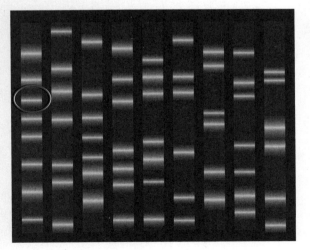

The Redhead Murders (pages 119–120)
1. B; 2. Tennessee and Kentucky; 3. C

Tracing the Suspect (page 121)
The order is: Krakow, Poland; Prague, Czech Republic; Rabat, Morocco; Antananarivo, Madagascar; Kuala Lumpur, Malaysia; Singapore; Barcelona, Spain; Quito, Ecuador

Measuring Up (page 122)
1. c) 5½ yards
2. b) 3 land miles
3. b) 1 ounce
4. b) 8 quarts
5. a) 1 scruple
6. b) 40 yards
7. c) 200 milligrams
8. b) 18 inches
9. d) 4 inches
10. a) ⅙ inch
11. c) 500 sheets
12. c) 9 inches

Find the Witness (page 123)
The Wests live in house D.

Answers

Where'd the Money Go?
(page 124)

On the evening of November 24, 1971, a man calling himself Dan Cooper (later known as D. B. Cooper) hijacked an airplane, and demanded $200,000 and four parachutes, which he received when the plane landed in Seattle. Cooper allowed the plane's passengers to disembark but then ordered the pilot to fly to Mexico. Once the plane had gained enough altitude, somewhere over the Cascade Mountains near Woodland, Washington, Cooper jumped from the plane and fell into history. Despite a massive manhunt, no trace of him has ever been found. In 1980, an eight-year-old boy found nearly $6,000 in rotting $20 bills lying along the banks of the Columbia River. A check of their serial numbers found that they were part of the ransom money given to Cooper, but what became of the rest of the money, and Cooper, is a mystery to this day.

What Changed? (pages 125–126)
A bullet casing disappeared.

The Golden State Killer
(pages 127–128)
1. A; 2. C; 3. B

DNA Sequence (page 129)

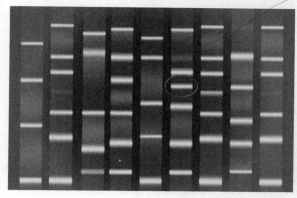

Jean Racine on Crime (page 130)
Crime like virtue has its degrees; and timid innocence was never known to blossom suddenly into extreme license.

Resolving Crime (page 130)
The only medicine for suffering, crime, and all the other woes of mankind, is wisdom.

Seen at the Scene (pages 131–132)
Picture 3 is a match.

Orner and Freiburger (pages 133–134)
1. C; 2. A; 3. D

What Changed? (pages 135–136)
The person to the right of the tree walked away.

DNA Sequence (page 137)
They are a match.

Unlock the Safe (page 138)
58931

Answers

Three Quotes on Crime
(page 139)

The greatest of evils and the worst of crime is poverty.
—George Bernard Shaw

While there is a lower class I am in it, while there is a criminal element I am of it; while there is a soul in prison, I am not free.
—Eugene Victor Debs

Here is the charming evening, the criminal's friend.
—Charles Baudelaire

Marked Bills (pages 140–141)

Dates	Serials	Locations	Denominations
April 1	G-718428	Torbin	$50
April 5	F-667280	Midvale	$100
April 9	B-492841	Uteville	$5
April 13	C-918303	Nettleton	$10
April 17	P-101445	Finsberg	$20

DNA Sequence (page 142)
They are a match.

Double Murder (pages 143–144)
1. C; 2. B; 3. A

What Changed? (pages 145–146)
A flattened paper cup (center of picture, to the right of the case) disappeared.

A Notorious Murder (page 147)
In the early hours of March 9, 1997, influential rap artist Christopher Wallace, also known as Biggie Smalls or Notorious B.I.G., was gunned down by a drive-by shooter outside the Petersen Automotive Museum on Wilshire Boulevard. Wallace was at the museum to attend the after-party for "Vibe" magazine's Soul Train Music Awards. At around 12:30 A.M., Wallace left the event with his entourage. When his vehicle stopped at a red light just 50 yards from the museum, a black Chevy Impala pulled alongside, and the driver fired numerous rounds from a 9mm pistol, hitting the 24-year-old rap star in the chest. His murder remains unsolved, although plenty of conspiracy theories surround his death.

The Suspect's Escape Route
(page 148)

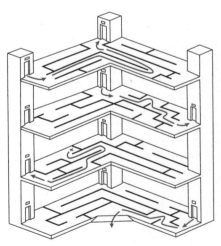

Seen at the Scene (pages 149–150)
Picture 3 is a match.

Answers

DNA Sequence (page 151)
They are a match.

Stolen Street Signs (pages 152-153)

Dates	Signs	Streets	Streets
July 4th	One Way	Dwight St.	Ralston Ave.
July 11th	Speed Limit	Casper Blvd.	Tarragon Ln.
July 18th	Dead End	Amble Ln.	Quinella St.
July 25th	Yield	Barnacle Rd.	Selby St.
August 1st	Stop	Falstaff St.	Oracle Rd.
August 8th	No Parking	Everett Ave.	Peabody Ln.

Find the Witness (page 154)
Perez lives in house D.

Justice at Last (pages 155-156)
1. C; 2. A; 3. B

Overheard Information
(pages 157-158)
1. D; 2. C; 3. B

DNA Sequence (page 159)

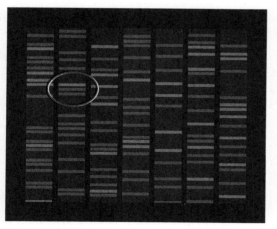

Finally Solved (page 160)
In June 1990, a driver for the Armored Motor Service of America (AMSA) and his female partner stopped for breakfast at a convenience store near Rochester, New York. While the female guard went into the store, a band of armed thieves attacked the driver, waited for the female guard to return, then ordered them to drive the truck to an unnamed location, where the thieves transferred the money to a waiting van, tied up the two guards, and escaped with the money. The total haul of $10.8 million ranked as one the largest heists in history. The robbery was also noteworthy for the fact that it remained unsolved for more than a decade. In 2002, though, the driver of the robbed AMSA truck, Albert Ranieri, admitted to masterminding the scheme.

What Changed? (pages 161-162)
One bottle on the middle shelf disappeared.

The Suspect's Escape Route
(page 163)

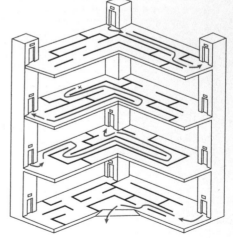

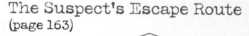

COLD CASES

Answers

What Is History? (page 164)
History is no more than the portrayal of crimes and misfortunes.

Crime in Poetry (page 164)
He left a corsair's name to other times,
Linked with one virtue, and a thousand crimes.

The Expanding Case of Samuel Little (pages 165–166)
1. D; 2. B; 3. A

Seen at the Scene (pages 167–168)
Picture 4 is a match.

From Opened to Closed (page 169)
Answers may vary. OPENED, opined, opines, spines, spires, spares, stares, stared, stored, stowed, slowed, glowed, gloved, gloves, cloves, closes, CLOSED

DNA Sequence (page 170)

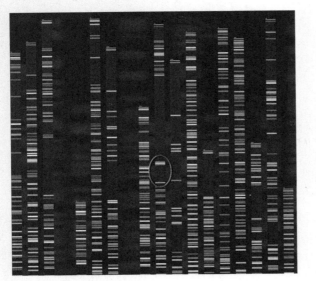

What Changed? (pages 171–172)
The shape of the evidence bag on the right changed.

Unlock the Safe (page 173)
70954

Find the Witness (page 174)
Shah lives in house A.

Seen at the Scene (pages 175–176)
Picture 1 is a match.

Fingerprint Match (page 177)
E, L, and N are the matching fingerprints.

Fingerprint Match (page 178)
The thief is in room 11.

COLD CASES